BEGINNERS' SPANISH

An Introduction to Conversational Spanish

Beginners' Spanish

An Introduction to Conversational Spanish

Terry Wilson

with illustrations by
Maureen Williams

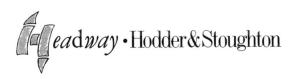

Headway · Hodder & Stoughton

ISBN 0 340 16354 2
First published 1976
Eighth impression 1989

Printed in Great Britain for Hodder and Stoughton Educational,
a division of Hodder and Stoughton Ltd, London, by
Page Bros (Norwich) Ltd

Contents

Structures: ¿Qué es? Es té/un vaso/una taza. ¿Es esto té (etc.)? No, es vino (etc.) ¿Qué son? Son vasos (etc.) ¿Son estos galletas (etc.)? Sí, señor, son galletas. No, señor (etc.), no son galletas (etc.) ¿Quiere Vd. una taza de té (etc.)?

Simple statements about refreshments, negation of verbs, questions, the indefinite article.

Structures: Es caro/cara. Son caros/caras. ¿Vd./el señor/él es inglés (etc.)? ¿Vd./la señora/ella es inglesa (etc.)? ¿Vds. (etc.) son ingleses/-as? Yo soy inglés (etc.) (1, 2 sing. and pl.) ¿Vd. (etc.) habla español? Lo hablo. Un hombre entra (etc.) ¿Vd. fuma (etc.)? Hablo mucho (etc.) Buenos días (etc.)

Definite article. Adjectives. Present tense -ar verbs. Subject pronouns and their omission. Lo.

Structures: Los señores llegan. Los señores no bajan. Miran el libro. Hay un bar en el aeropuerto. ¿Hay un bar . . . ? ¿Qué hace el mozo? Un libro inglés. Un buen libro. El libro es bueno. Me gusta el té. No me gusta . . . ¿No le gusta . . . ?

Third person plural of verbs. Position of adjectives: apocopation. Gustar.

Structures: El señor está en el bar. Está *and preposition, etc.* Quiero/voy a/ me gusta/hablar.

Ser and estar. The infinitive. Stress mark on question word.

Introduction

This book is designed to fit alongside the successful *Beginners' French*, *Beginners' German* and *Beginners' Italian*, and in broad outline follows the plan of these works.

It is intended for adult beginners of Spanish, principally in Adult Education classes but also for those studying Spanish without a teacher.

It is based upon considerable practical experience in the teaching of Modern Languages. Its primary bias is towards the spoken language as the basis for further study.

The ability to speak a language cannot be gained from grammar study or reading, but like any other skill it can be acquired only through systematic and diligent practice. This book provides material for such practice and presents it in such a way that memorising and assimilation are facilitated.

After an introduction to the pronunciation of Spanish, which should be read carefully and referred back to at stages throughout the study of the book, sixteen lessons follow.

Each lesson starts with a series of pictures accompanied by sentences which illustrate one of the main grammatical points of the lesson. Next, there is a dialogue. This and the preceding sentences should be committed to memory, as the great majority of the sentences used will serve as models for the formation of numerous other sentences (as shown in the *Fluency Practice* tables which occur later), and others present common conversational expressions.

After the picture section and the dialogue comes a list of new words which are not listed elsewhere in the chapter, or which might cause problems of understanding in the dialogues. The student is recommended to make a separate vocabulary list, as writing helps to fix the spelling in the mind. However, the danger of too great a dependence on translation must be stressed: a language cannot be learnt by translating an English sentence word by word, and the best results are obtained by learning whole sentences and practising the basic grammatical structures by means of slotting in alternative expressions which follow the basic structures of the foreign language, rather than those of English.

It is for this reason that so much stress is laid on the Fluency Practice sections. The structural practice obtained by working through these makes the production of correct sentences second nature rather than a demanding intellectual feat. The method of use is simple. Any element from the left of a vertical line will combine with any element from the right of it to produce a grammatically correct sentence. First, a simple example: it will readily be seen that the sentences *Es té, Es café, Es queso, Es un vaso, Es una taza* can all be produced from Chapter 1, Fluency Practice Item 1. The horizontal lines separate and must not be crossed: hence, from the same table *un* can be placed with *vaso, cuchillo, tenedor, bocadillo* but not with *taza, botella, cuchara, galleta* which demand *una*. The student should practise all the combinations possible. A slightly more complicated example from Chapter 14 will show that two of the possible sentences are *Tocabas mucho el piano cuando tenías ocho años* (You used to play the piano a lot when you were eight years old) and *Jugabas al fútbol cuando llegué* (You were playing football when I arrived).

This technique makes the production of correct sentences much easier than by memorising grammatical rules and remembering to apply them. However, it is felt that in a course of this kind some explanations are necessary, and these follow the Fluency Practice sections. Every effort has been made to keep them short and to use the minimum of grammatical terminology.

Each chapter has a series of additional exercises designed to give further practice in the use of the points studied. Translation has been avoided except for points which English-speaking students find particularly difficult because of basic differences in the structure of the two languages. The student is sometimes given guidance in the writing of material involving re-use of points from the lesson: here it is essential that the student should operate by selecting from the picture texts, dialogues and fluency practice sections suitable phrases to combine into a flowing passage rather than to work out in English what is to be said and then try to translate it. The student without a teacher should try hard to get in touch with Spanish speakers through local or national societies and institutions to correct any such work.

Finally, there is an index which permits the location of material for revision purposes.

The author wishes to thank Mr Joseph Harvard, Mrs Soledad Sprackling, Mrs. Jane Johnson and Mrs. Sarah Boas for their patient help and encouragement.

Pronunciation Guide

No book can teach pronunciation: a language is primarily spoken, and educated native speakers are the most reliable guide. The student should seek out opportunities of meeting native speakers and hearing Spanish spoken on the radio and on film and sound recordings.

It is necessary, however, to give guidance on pronunciation and the following will be found helpful.

There are fewer different sounds in Spanish than in English, and the spelling system is much simpler. The pronunciation of a sound in Spanish is to all intents and purposes not affected by stress. Hence there are no difficulties such as those arising in English from the different pronunciations of the group 'ar' occurring in the words 'part', 'particular' and 'warm', the different values of letter 'a' in 'late', 'hat', 'attentive', 'banana', etc., or silent letters, such as the 'e' in 'late'.

A list of sounds follows: unless there is a remark to the contrary, the explanation given is valid for the accepted speech form, educated Castilian Spanish. The major variations found in the South and in South America are listed for information to avoid confusion when hearing speakers from those regions, but no attempt is made to give any sort of detail on regional variations other than those which could cause confusion.

VOWELS

Each has one sound only, which should not be varied from word to word or position to position. The student should be careful not to weaken the vowel when it is unstressed (see *Stressing*) and should try to keep the position of the teeth, lips, and tongue the same throughout the pronunciation of a vowel (the English tendency is to diphthongise).

A   *taza, azúcar, vaso, agua, azafata, cerveza.* This falls between 'a' in 'apple' and 'ar' in 'arm'.

E   *es, esto, de, cerveza, botella, café, leche.* This closely resembles the 'e' in 'egg'. Avoid diphthongisation: *de* does not rhyme with the English word 'day'.

I   *vino, bocadillo, sí, gracias, señorita.* The 'i' in 'machine' is near, but the teeth should be closer together, the lips nearer a smile, and the sound made tighter than in English by raising the tongue more.

O *botella, vaso, esto, bocadillo, señor, son, favor.* In between the 'o' in 'on' and 'fork' in terms of length. An open 'o'—avoid the 'o' from English 'rose'.

U *un, una, azúcar, agua, cuchillo, cuchara.* Standard English 'put', 'good' and 'look' come near to it; northern 'by gum' is better from some points of view. It cannot be pronounced with the lips *flat*, so look in a mirror and push the lips forward while rounding them slightly—you can't smile while doing this. In *agua* the sound is nearer to an English 'w' as in 'wag': this is the value between **g** and **a** or **o**. Between **g** and **e** or **i** it hardens the **g** (see below) but is not pronounced.

Y equivalent to 'i'. As a consonant, like English 'y', e.g. *ya* as in 'yellow'.

CONSONANTS

B In Spanish, equivalent to the letter **V**. As the first letter in a word, quite like the English 'b' but softer, less explosive: *vaso, bocadillo, vino, barato, bueno, bien.* Between vowels a cross between an English 'b' and 'v' but made with both lips, not lip against teeth. If in doubt, pronounce as a 'b': *cerveza, favor.* In other positions, as in the initial position: *hombre, nombre, habla, amable.*

C Before **e** or **i**, like English 'th' in 'thing': *cerveza, gracias, cigarrillo, escocesa, acento.* Many Southern and South American speakers pronounce this exactly as they do **s**. In other positions except **CH** (regarded as a separate letter of the alphabet), sounds like a 'k' or English 'c' in 'cup': *café, azúcar, bocadillo, cuchillo, cuchara, caro.*

CH Quite like English 'ch' in 'church': *leche, chocolate, churro, mucho, muchacho.*

D Initially and in many combinations, quite like English 'd': *de, día, tarde, del, delante* (but some speakers always pronounce it as 'th' in English 'the'). Between vowels it usually has the sound of 'th' in English 'the', but in this position, particularly between **a** and **o**, you will notice that many speakers omit it completely: *bocadillos, nada, pescado, tenedor, estudio.* At the end of a word, it can sound like 'th' in 'the' or 'thing': *Madrid, usted,* or be omitted. (The student should pronounce it.)

F Like English 'f': *café, azafata, favor, feo, fuma.*

G Before **a**, **o** or **u** or a consonant, as in English 'go': *galletas, agua, gracias, tengo, inglés.*

Before **e** or **i**, like Spanish **j**. There is no such sound in standard

English, but the 'ch' in Scottish 'loch' comes near. Southern and South American speakers pronounce it rather like English 'h' as in 'heat'. Example: *general, gente, inteligente*. See also **J**.

H Is silent: *hermoso, hombre, hablo, hay, hace, helado*.

J In all positions like Spanish **g** before **e** and **i**: *pasajero, mujer, mejicano, baja, juguete*.

K Hardly used but like English 'k'; only likely to be encountered in *kilo* and combinations of it like *kilogramo, kilómetro* and foreign-based words like *kirie, Kodak* and *Kremlin*.

L Like an English 'l' as in 'letter' but never as in 'skittle' or 'bill': *leche, español, amable, claro, inglés*. See **LL**.

LL A separate letter of the alphabet in Spanish: quite like the combination 'li' in 'Italian', but longer, except in the South and South America where it sounds like the 'y' in 'yellow': *botella, bocadillo, galleta, mantequilla, cuchillo*.

M Like English 'm': *también, más, mantequilla, mucho, amable*.

N Like English 'n': *vino, también, con, nada, pan*. The student will probably notice a tendency for Spaniards to pronounce it like the 'n' in 'bank' (i.e. with a sort of 'g' sound following it) in some combinations before a vowel: '*en el banco*' might appear to have a 'g' between *en* and *el*. In combinations like *enviar* it can sound like an 'm'. See **Ñ**.

Ñ A separate letter of the alphabet. Like 'n' plus 'y' as in 'yellow': *señorita, señor, español, España, araña*.

P Quite like the English 'p'. However, most English people aspirate the 'p' (i.e., follow it closely with a little puff of breath, which will flicker the edge of a piece of paper or a flame, or sound like an explosion when speaking too close to a microphone) when it starts a word, coming immediately before a vowel: this should not occur in Spanish except under strain conditions (e.g. shouting). Spaniards will understand the English 'p' but the student should try to be less explosive: the student hearing Spanish may occasionally mistake a **p** for a **b**, which is not normally aspirated in standard English. Examples: *pasajero, por, pan, lápiz, guapo*.

Q Always followed by a silent **u**. Has the sound of 'k'. Examples: *¿qué?, quiere, quien, porque, quiosco*.

R (to be distinguished from **RR**). Pronounced with the tip of the tongue, only slightly rolled: the teeth do not usually bite as with many English speakers. Because the trill is very short, English people may tend to hear it as a **d** but practice will soon help in distinguishing between the two sounds.

Another problem about the Spanish **r** is that it is always pronounced, whereas '-r' following a vowel in Standard English changes the vowel sound and is silent. Thus the 'r' in the English 'cart' is usually silent and the 'a' is not the same sound as in 'cat'. In Spanish **dar** is pronounced as **d** followed by an unchanged **a** followed by a pronounced **r**. This is very important. Here are some examples:

(a) **r** in the middle of the word: *periódico, caramelo, mira, pulsera*;

(b) **r** at the end of the word: *azúcar, señor, por favor*, and infinitives such as *hablar, comer, vivir, dar*;

(c) **r** with consonants: *compra, siempre, abre, ofrece, escribe*;

(d) Initial **r**. This counts as **RR** (see below). *Rusia, reír, revista.*

RR This is considered as a separate letter and is very strongly rolled (trilled) with the tip of the tongue. It only occurs between vowels. Contrast: *pero, perro; caro, carro; cigarrillo, churro, burro.*

S Quite like the English 's' as in 'sad'. E.g. *esto, vaso, es, nos, galletas.* The tip of the tongue is usually further back than in English, giving a slurred quality approaching the English 'sh' at times. Before some voiced consonants (**b, d, m**) **s** is pronounced as in the English 'rose'. E.g. *mismo.*

T Like the English 't' but not aspirated in the initial position (see **P**), pronounced with the tongue less far forward and is therefore less explosive than the English sound. Examples: *té, esto, también, taza.*

V Is pronounced like **B** (q.v.). Although having the same sound they are not interchangeable at will in spelling.

X Like the English 'x' as in 'ex' but not as in 'exempt'. It is not very common in Spanish. However, the prefix ex- is very common and is pronounced as **es**: *explicación, excursión.*

Y As a consonant like the English 'y' as in 'yellow'.

Z Like English 'th' ('thin'): *taza, cerveza, azúcar, lápiz.* Many Southerners and South Americans pronounce it as **s**.

ORTHOGRAPHIC CHANGES

These affect mainly **c-z**, **g-gu**, and **c-qu**.

Spanish **ce** and **ci** are pronounced with a **c** that has the same sound as Spanish **z**. In writing, **ce** and **ci** are preferred to **ze**, **zi**. The singular noun *lápiz* has the plural form *lápices* as a result.

G and **C** before **-a, -o, -u** are 'hard'. If they are part of the stem (root) of a verb, their sound has to be preserved if the ending changes to include an **-e** or **-i**. Example: verb *juzgar*, in a form which ends in *-e*, *juzgue*. The *u*, not pronounced, is written to avoid the *ge* pronunciation. Likewise, *buscar* with *-e* ending becomes *busque* so as not to alter the pronunciation to *ce*.

COMBINATIONS OF VOWELS

Vowels in combination are pronounced as written, without pause between, according to these rules:

1 **A, E, O** are considered 'strong', **I, U** are considered 'weak'.

2 Strong vowels together count as one syllable each. *Fea* is therefore a two-syllable word in which each vowel keeps its value as explained above. *Poema* has three syllables.

3 Weak vowels together form a diphthong with the stress on the second vowel. *Viuda* therefore has two syllables with the stress on *u*. (See *Stressing* below).

4 A strong vowel combined with a weak vowel or vowels bears the stress and the combination counts as one syllable. *Quiere* therefore has two syllables, with the stress on the first *e*. *Bueno* has two syllables and the stress is on the *e*.

5 A word may be pronounced with the stress on a weak vowel in a vowel combination in two sets of circumstances:
   a) where the weak vowel is marked with a stress-mark: *mayoría*.
   b) in certain verb forms which do not now need the stressed ending to be marked: infinitive ending *-air, -eir, -oir*;
   certain monosyllabic verb forms, e.g. *fui, dio*.

STRESSING

Spanish, like English, has a clear contrast between stressed and unstressed syllables. Its stressing system is much more regular and therefore easier to learn. (The problem for English speakers of Spanish is to maintain the value of the vowels in the unstressed position, as was pointed out at the beginning of the pronunciation section.) The rules are as follows:

1 Words ending in a vowel or combination of vowels: the stress falls on the next to last syllable. *Esto, vaso, leche, botella, galleta, bocadillo, quiere*. The vast majority of Spanish words fall into this class.

2 Plural form of such words formed by adding *-s* (nouns, adjectives) or *-n* (verbs): the stress is maintained in the same position, therefore *estos*, *vasos*, *quieren*, etc.

3 Words ending in *-s* or *-n* are usually stressed on the next to last syllable.

4 Words ending in a consonant other than *-s* or *-n*: the stress falls on the last syllable: *señor*, *favor*, *español*, *usted*.

5 There are certain exceptions to these rules, but in such cases an acute accent is always placed over the syllable where the stress falls. An exception to rule 1 is *café*; the accent must be used. An exception to rule 3 is *alemán*, but when *alemán* takes a vowel (f) *alemana*, or itself becomes plural by the addition of *-es* (*alemanes*), the original rules take over, so the accent is no longer written. An exception to rule 4 is *fácil*.

6 When a word stressed on the next to last syllable itself becomes plural, the stress is maintained in the original position by the use of the accent if the stressing does not alter, hence: *orden*, *órdenes*.

USES OF THE ACCENT (STRESS-MARK) NOT AFFECTING PRONUNCIATION

To differentiate between words of identical spelling but different function: *el*, the; *él*, he; *si*, if; *sí*, yes.

Also to add additional marking to the interrogative and exclamatory form of pronouns and adverbs:

    como how   *¿cómo?* how?

It is also used to distinguish between otherwise identical forms of demonstrative pronouns (*éste*) and demonstrative adjectives (*este libro*). Further treatment of this subject is unnecessary for the scope of the present course, but the student should know, when he comes to read original Spanish texts, that the rules have been changing over the centuries and that the last official revision took place in 1952, hence he will meet apparent anomalies.

INTONATION

The rise and fall of the voice in Spanish does not closely resemble that of English. On the whole it is true to say that statements end low in both languages, as do questions beginning with a question word, but that other questions rise at the end. The fall of the voice at the end of word-groups, often represented by a comma in print, typical of English, is not mirrored in Spanish. While correct intonation is perhaps more important than correct pronunciation for the purposes of being understood, it would be impossible to treat it adequately in a work as brief as this. The student should listen closely to the intonation of live speakers and to recordings, paying attention to the total context and trying gradually to build up ideas about what sounds polite, brusque, or downright rude to a Spanish speaker, since the intonative patterns of the two languages do not match closely.

SINALEFA

In Spanish no pause is made between words within a sense-group. No separation should be made between words when one ends with a vowel and the next begins with a vowel: e.g. Esto es, té o café, ¿qué es?, la azafata, ¿habla usted?, no es, está el, ve a un, etc. The student is advised to study every text with this in mind.

PUNCTUATION

In Spanish punctuation is marked in the same way as in English, with the difference that interrogation and exclamation marks always occur at the beginning of the sentence as well as at the end. The marks at the beginning of the sentence are written upside down. For example:

—¿Tiene,Vd. caramelos, por favor?—preguntó.
("Have you any sweets, please?" he asked.)

Dialogues are usually contained within dashes, for each individual speech.

There are slight differences between the use of commas in English and Spanish, but these need not concern us at this stage.

Capitals:

Nouns and adjectives denoting nationality begin with a small letter, as do those connected with towns and regions. Similarly, the names of days and months are not usually written with capitals. Names of bodies and societies, and titles also have small letters.

ABBREVIATIONS USED IN THIS BOOK

E	=	Explanations
FP	=	Fluency Practice
m	=	masculine
f	=	feminine
s	=	singular
pl	=	plural

Numerals

1	uno, una	25	veinticinco, veinte y cinco
2	dos	26	veintiséis, veinte y seis
3	tres	27	veintisiete, veinte y siete
4	cuatro	28	veintiocho, veinte y ocho
5	cinco	29	veintinueve, veinte y nueve
6	seis	30	treinta
7	siete	32	treinta y uno
8	ocho	40	cuarenta
9	nueve	50	cincuenta
10	diez	60	sesenta
11	once	70	setenta
12	doce	80	ochenta
13	trece	90	noventa
14	catorce	100	ciento (cien)
15	quince	101	ciento uno, una
16	dieciséis	120	ciento veinte
17	diecisiete	135	ciento treinta y cinco
18	dieciocho	200	doscientos, doscientas
19	diecinueve	300	trescientos, -as
20	veinte	600	seiscientos, -as
21	veintiuno, veintiuna, veinte y uno	900	novecientos, -as
		1,000	mil
22	veintidós, veinte y dos	1,100	mil ciento
23	veintitrés, veinte y tres	2,000	dos mil
24	veinticuatro, veinte y cuatro	1,000,000	un millón

Lección Primera

A Esto es un vaso de cerveza.

B Esto es una botella de vino.

C Esto es un vaso de agua.

D Esto es una taza de café.

E Esto es leche.

F Esto es azúcar.

G Estos son galletas.   H Estos son bocadillos.

EN EL AVIÓN

Pasajero:	Señorita, ¿es esto té o café?
Azafata:	Es café, señor.
Pasajero:	¿Es esto cerveza?
Azafata:	Sí, señor.
Pasajero:	¿Es esto también cerveza?
Azafata:	No, señor, no es cerveza, es vino.
Pasajero:	Y esto, ¿qué es, por favor?
Azafata:	Es leche, señor.
Pasajero:	Y ¿qué son estos?
Azafata:	Son galletas, señor.
Pasajero:	Una taza de café con galletas, por favor, señorita.
Azafata:	¿Café con leche, señor?
Pasajero:	No, gracias, café solo.
Azafata:	¿Quiere Vd. azúcar, señor?
Pasajero:	Sí, por favor. Gracias, señorita.
Azafata:	De nada, señor. ¿Quiere Vd. algo más, señor?
Pasajero:	No, gracias, señorita.

un avión – *an aeroplane*
un pasajero – *a passenger*
la azafata – *air hostess*
¿es esto . . . ? – *is this . . . ?*
(*see E2*)
sí – *yes*
también – *also*
y – *and*
¿qué es? – *what is it?*
por favor – *please*

¿qué son? – *what are?*
café con leche – *white coffee*
gracias – *thank you*
café solo – *black coffee*
de nada – *don't mention it,
not at all*
algo más – *something else*
¿quiere Vd.? – *do you want?*
(*see FP5 and E1*)

3

FLUENCY PRACTICE

1

¿ Qué es ?			*What is it ?*		
Es	té		*It's*	*tea*	
	café			*coffee*	
	vino			*wine*	
	leche			*milk*	
	agua			*water*	
	pan			*bread*	
	carne			*meat*	
	pescado			*fish*	
	azúcar			*sugar*	
	mantequilla			*butter*	
	chocolate			*chocolate*	
	queso			*cheese*	
	un	vaso		*a*	*glass*
		cuchillo			*knife*
		tenedor			*fork*
		bocadillo			*sandwich*
	una	taza			*cup*
		botella			*bottle*
		cuchara			*spoon*
		galleta			*biscuit*

2a

¿ Es esto	té ?		*Is this*	*tea ?*	
	café ?			*coffee ?*	
	leche ?			*milk ?*	
	un	cuchillo ?		*a*	*knife ?*
		bocadillo ?			*sandwich ?*
		pasajero ?			*passenger ?*
	una	cuchara ?			*spoon ?*
		galleta ?			*biscuit ?*
		azafata ?			*an air hostess ?*

2b

Es	vino		*It is*	*wine*	
No es	leche		*It isn't*	*milk*	
	cerveza			*beer*	
	un	cuchillo		*a*	*knife*
		bocadillo			*sandwich*
		tenedor			*fork*
		lápiz			*pencil*
	una	cuchara			*spoon*
		galleta			*biscuit*
		botella			*bottle*

4

3

¿Qué son?		*What are they?*	
Son	vasos	*They are*	*glasses*
	cuchillos		*knives*
	bocadillos		*sandwiches*
	tenedores		*forks*
	lápices		*pencils*
	galletas		*biscuits*
	botellas de vino		*bottles of wine*
	pasajeros		*passengers*
	azafatas		*air hostesses*

4a

¿Son estos	galletas?	*Are these*	*biscuits?*
	bocadillos?		*sandwiches?*
	tazas de café?		*cups of coffee?*
	botellas de cerveza?		*bottles of beer?*

4b

Sí,	señor,	son	galletas	*Yes,*	*Sir,*	*they are*	*biscuits*
No,	señora,	no son	bocadillos	*No,*	*Madam,*	*they aren't*	*sandwiches*
	señorita,		etc.		*Miss,*		*etc.*

5

¿Quiere Vd.	una taza de té?	*Do you want a*	*a cup of tea?*
	un vaso de cerveza?	*Would you like*	*a glass of beer?*
	más azúcar?		*more sugar?*
	algo más?		*something else?*
	más galletas?		*more biscuits?*

EXPLANATIONS

1 *Vd.* is the usual abbreviation for *usted*, the word for 'you' when speaking to strangers and adults with whom we are not on very familiar terms.

2 *Es* means 'is' but also stands for 'it is'. Similarly, *son* (are) also stands for 'they are'. (*Es* used with *Vd.* has the meaning of 'are').

3 *No* used before a verb makes it negative: e.g. *no es vino* (it isn't wine), *no son galletas* (they aren't biscuits).

4 ¿ indicates the beginning of a question.

5 The indefinite article ('a' or 'an') is *un* before a masculine noun and *una* before a feminine noun.

All Spanish nouns are either masculine or feminine; these terms do not mean the same as 'male' and 'female'. Nouns ending in -*o* are usually masculine and nouns ending in -*a* are usually feminine.

6 The plural of a noun ending in -*o* or -*a* is formed by adding -*s*. Nouns ending in a consonant add -*es*: e.g. *un tenedor* (a fork); *tenedores* (forks). N.B. *lápiz* – *lápices:* an orthographic change (see *Pronunciation*).

5

EXERCISES *Look at the pictures on page 2.*

1 A ¿ Qué es esto ?   E ¿ Qué es esto ?
  B ¿ Qué es esto ?   F ¿ Qué es esto ?
  C ¿ Qué es esto ?   G ¿ Qué son estos ?
  D ¿ Qué es esto ?   H ¿ Qué son estos ?

2 A ¿ Es esto un vaso de cerveza ?
      Sí, es un vaso de cerveza.
  B ¿ Es esto una botella de cerveza ?
      No, es una botella de vino.
  C ¿ Es esto un vaso de agua ? Sí, . . .
  D ¿ Es esto azúcar ? No, . . .
  E ¿ Es esto leche ?
  F ¿ Es esto café ?
  G ¿ Son estos galletas ?
  H ¿ Son estos bocadillos ?

3 *Look at the pictures below and answer the question:* ¿ qué son ?

4 A ¿Son azafatas?
  B ¿Son cuchillos?
  C ¿Son pasajeros?
  D ¿Son tenedores?
  E ¿Son lápices?
  F ¿Son vasos?
  G ¿Son galletas?
  H ¿Son bocadillos?

5 Ask a Spanish guest if he would like tea or coffee.
                              sugar and milk.
                              a sandwich.
                              some biscuits.
                              more of what he is drinking.
                              something else.
                              more biscuits.

(NB In exercises of this type restrict yourself entirely to expressions taken from the course.)

Lección Dos

A Es barato.

B Es caro.

C Es barata.

D Es cara.

E Es feo.

F Es fea.

G Es guapo.

H Es guapa.

J Son baratos.

K Son caras.

¿VD. FUMA, SEÑOR?

El español: Buenas tardes, señor. ¿Habla Vd. español?

El inglés: No muy bien, señor. ¿Habla Vd. inglés?

El español: Muy poco, señor.

El norteamericano: ¿Vd. fuma, señor?

El inglés: Gracias, no fumo.

El norteamericano: ¿Y Vd., señor?

El español: Con mucho gusto. Vd. es muy amable. ¿Es un cigarrillo inglés, no?

El norteamericano: No, señor, es un cigarrillo norteamericano.

El español: Son buenos. ¿Es Vd. norteamericano, señor?

El norteamericano: Sí, soy norteamericano.

El español: Y Vd., señor, ¿es también norteamericano?

El inglés: No, señor, no soy norteamericano. Soy inglés, pero mi mujer no es inglesa. Es escocesa.

El español: ¿Así habla inglés con acento escocés?

El inglés: Sí, claro. Aun habla español con acento escocés.

¿Vd. fuma? – *do you smoke?*	amable – *kind*
(*see FP9 and E8*)	un cigarrillo – *cigarette*
¿habla Vd.? – *do you speak?*	pero – *but*
(*see FP7*)	mi mujer – *my wife*
muy – *very*	así – *so, thus*
bien – *well*	un acento – *an accent*
poco – *little*	claro – *of course*
con mucho gusto – *with much pleasure*	aun – *even*

FLUENCY PRACTICE

1

Es	caro barato guapo feo bueno malo	He/it is	expensive cheap handsome ugly good bad	(referring to masculine person or thing)
	cara barata guapa fea buena mala	She/it is	expensive cheap handsome, good-looking ugly good bad	(feminine person or thing)

2

¿ Vd.		es	inglés?	Are you		English?*
¿ El	señor mozo hombre muchacho profesor alumno		escocés? irlandés? francés? español? alemán? italiano?	Is the	gentleman waiter man boy teacher pupil	Scottish? Irish? French? Spanish? German? Italian?
¿ Él			norteamericano? sudamericano? australiano?	Is he		American? South American? Australian?

*or 'an Englishman' etc.

3

¿ Vd.		es	inglesa?	Are you		English?*
¿ La	señora moza mujer muchacha profesora alumna		escocesa? irlandesa? francesa? española? alemana? italiana?	Is the	lady waitress woman girl teacher pupil	Scottish? Irish? French? Spanish? German? Italian?
¿ Ella			norteamericana? sudamericana? australiana?	Is she		American? South American? Australian?

*or 'an Englishwoman' etc.

4

¿ Vds.		son	ingleses ?	Are you		English ?
¿ Los	señores		franceses ?	Are the	gentlemen	French ?
	mozos		españoles ?		waiters	Spanish ?
	alumnos		italianos ?		pupils	Italian ?
	muchachos		americanos ?		boys	South American ?
	profesores		portugueses ?		teachers	Portuguese ?
¿ Ellos			suecos ?	Are they (m.)		Swedish ?

5

¿ Vds.		son	inglesas ?	Are you		English ?
¿ Las	señoras		francesas ?	Are the	ladies	French ?
	mozas		españolas ?		waitresses	Spanish ?
	alumnas		italianas ?		pupils	Italian ?
	muchachas		americanas ?		girls	South American ?
	profesoras		portuguesas ?		teachers	Portuguese ?
¿ Ellas			suecas ?	Are they (f.)		Swedish ?

6

Yo soy	inglés	I am	English	
Vd. es	español	You are	Spanish	(masculine)
Él es	francés	He is	French	
Yo soy	inglesa	I am	English	
Vd. es	española	You are	Spanish	(feminine)
Ella es	francesa	She is	French	
Nosotros somos	ingleses	We are	English	
Vds. son	españoles	You are	Spanish	(masculine)
Ellos son	franceses	They are	French	
Nosotras somos	inglesas	We are	English	
Vds. son	españolas	You are	Spanish	(feminine)
Ellas son	francesas	They are	French	

7a

¿ Vd.	habla	español ?	Do you		speak	Spanish ?
¿ El señor		inglés ?	Does the	gentleman		English ?
¿ La señora		francés ?		lady		French ?
¿ El muchacho		italiano ?		boy		Italian ?
¿ La muchacha		alemán ?		girl		German ?
¿ El mozo		portugués ?		waiter		Portuguese ?
¿ La moza		holandés ?		waitress		Dutch ?
¿ Quién			Who		speaks	

11

Sí, lo hablo	Yes, I speak it
No, no lo hablo	No, I don't speak it
Sí, lo habla	Yes, he/she speaks it
No, no lo habla	No, he/she doesn't speak it

Lo	hablo	un poco		I	speak	it	a little
	habla	muy bien		You			very well
		muy poco		He	speaks		very little
		bastante bien		She			quite well
		mal					badly

8

Un	hombre	entra		A	man	is	coming in
El	muchacho	baja		The	boy		coming down
	español	habla			Spaniard		speaking
	mejicano	canta			Mexican		singing
Él		baila		He			dancing
Una	mujer	escucha		A	woman		listening
La	muchacha	mira		The	girl		looking
	española	estudia			Spanish woman		studying
	mejicana	fuma			Mexican woman		smoking
Ella				She			

9

¿ Vd.	fuma?		Are you		smoking?
¿ El hombre	entra?		Is the	man	coming in?
muchacho	mira?			boy	looking?
inglés	baja?			Englishman	coming down?
¿ La mujer	canta?			woman	singing?
muchacha	baila?			girl	dancing?
francesa	escucha?			Frenchwoman	listening?
Sí, (yo)	fumo		Yes, I am		smoking
No, (yo) no	miro		No, I'm not		looking
Sí, (él) (ella)	entra		Yes, he/she is		coming in
No, (él) (ella) no	baja		No, he/she isn't		coming down
	etc.				etc.

10

hablo	mucho	I talk	a lot
canto	poco	sing	(very) little*
bailo	muy poco	dance	very little
estudio	bien	study	well
	mal		badly

* usually becomes negative in English: 'I don't talk (etc.) very much'.

11

Buenos	días	*Good*	*morning (day)*
Buenas	tardes		*afternoon*
	noches		*night*

EXPLANATIONS

1 The Definite Article ('the') has four forms in Spanish:
   el before a masculine noun, singular
   la before a feminine noun, singular*
   los before a masculine noun, plural
   las before a feminine noun, plural.
   * except before a stressed 'a': e.g. *el agua* (f) 'water'.

2 Adjectives agree in number and gender with the noun to which they refer. (See especially Fluency Practice tables 1 and 4)

3 Words denoting nationality do not start with a capital letter.

4 The distinction made in English between 'I smoke' and 'I am smoking' need not always be made in Spanish. *Fumo* can express both. Similarly, *no fumo* can mean both 'I don't smoke' and 'I am not smoking'. So *¿ Vd. fuma ?* can therefore mean 'Do you smoke?' or 'Are you smoking?'. (But see also Ch. 7).

5 As the endings of Spanish verbs indicate person and number, the subject pronouns (*yo*—'I', etc.) are usually omitted, unless needed for clarity or emphasis.

6 *Usted (Vd.)* originally meant 'Your Grace', so it is used with the third person (*es, fuma, habla*, etc.). It can be omitted. Its plural is *Ustedes (Vds.)*.

7 *Nosotros* and *ellos* are the masculine forms and *nosotras* and *ellas* are the feminine forms for 'we' and 'they'.

8 Questions can be formed with the same word order as used in statements, or the subject and verb can be transposed, e.g. *¿ Vd. fuma ?* or *¿ Fuma Vd. ?*, *¿ El inglés baja ?* or *¿ Baja el inglés ?* The English use of parts of 'to do' and 'to be' cannot be applied.

9 *Lo* (it). This masculine object pronoun precedes the finite verb in statements and questions.

EXERCISES

1 El señor Sánchez es español. Habla español, inglés y poco de francés. Fuma mucho. Baila con una inglesa, señorita Shaw. Él baila mal, pero ella baila bien.

La señorita Shaw es azafata. Canta muy bien, y no fuma. Habla inglés y francés, pero no habla español.

   1. El señor Sánchez, ¿es italiano?
   2. ¿Habla inglés?
   3. Y la señorita Shaw, ¿habla español?
   4. ¿Baila bien el señor Sánchez?
   5. ¿Baila bien la señorita Shaw?
   6. ¿Quién canta?
   7. ¿Quién fuma? ¿Fuma mucho o poco?
   8. ¿Quién no fuma?
   9. ¿Quién habla un poco de francés?
  10. La señorita Shaw, ¿es profesora?

2 You meet a Spaniard, and in the course of conversation he offers you a cigarette. You accept, and ask him if it is a Spanish one. He is travelling with two friends who are teachers: you ask if they are Spanish too. You offer him a drink of beer or wine.

Write out your side of the conversation, keeping to expressions learnt so far.

Lección Tres

A Los pasajeros bajan del avión.   B Entran en el aeropuerto.

C Hablan con el aduanero.   D Miran las revistas.

E Compran cigarrillos.   F Toman refrescos.

EN EL AEROPUERTO

El norteamericano: ¿Qué hacen el señor inglés y su mujer?

El español: Miran las revistas.

El norteamericano: ¿Son revistas españolas?

El español: Sí, son revistas españolas, pero también hay revistas inglesas, norteamericanas, francesas — de todas las nacionalidades. Además hay películas, cigarrillos, libros y juguetes.

15

El norteamericano: ¿Hay cigarrillos y libros norteamericanos?
El español: Sí, pero la mayoría son españoles.
El norteamericano: ¿Son buenos los cigarrillos españoles?
El español: Sí, son buenos, pero me gustan más los cigarrillos ingleses.

del avión – *from the plane*	todas – *all (f.pl.)*
en – *into, in*	nacionalidad – *nationality*
el aeropuerto – *the airport*	además – *besides*
el aduanero – *the customs officer*	hay – *there is, there are*
toman refrescos – *they are having refreshments*	películas – *films*
	libros – *books*
su mujer – *his wife*	juguetes – *toys (m.)*
revistas – *magazines*	la mayoría – *most*
	me gusta – *I like (see E4)*

FLUENCY PRACTICE

1

Los	señores mozos	llegan entran	The	gentlemen waiters	arrive come in
(Ellos)		hablan	They (m)		talk
Las	señoras mozas	miran escuchan	The	ladies waitresses	look listen
(Ellas) Vds.		fuman cantan bailan esperan bajan	They (f) You (pl)		smoke sing dance wait come down

Los señores *etc.*	no bajan	The gentlemen *etc.*	don't come down

Miran Compran	el	libro periódico	They are	looking at buying	the	book paper
Toman Aceptan	la	revista película		taking accepting		magazine film
	los	libros periódicos				books papers
	las	películas				films

No miran *etc.*	el libro	They aren't looking at *etc.*	the book

2

Hay	un bar	en	el aeropuerto	*There*	*is*	*a bar*	*in*	*the*	*airport*
	un restaurante		la estación			*a restaurant*			*station*
	una tienda		el puerto			*shop*			*port*
	bares		la plaza		*are*	*bars*			*square*
	restaurantes					*restaurants*			
	tiendas					*shops*			

¿ Hay	un bar	en el aeropuerto?	*Is there*	*a bar*	*in the airport?*
	bares	cerca de aquí?	*Are there*	*bars*	*near here?*
	etc.	*etc.*		*etc.*	*etc.*

3

¿ Qué	hace	el mozo?	*What is*	*the waiter*	*doing?*
	dice	la moza?		*waitress*	*saying?*
¿ Qué	hacen	los mozos?	*What are*	*the waiters*	*doing?*
	dicen	las mozas?		*waitresses*	*saying?*

4a

un	libro	inglés	*an*	*English*	*book*
	periódico	interesante		*interesting*	*newspaper*
		blanco	*a*	*white*	
		rojo		*red*	
		azul		*blue*	
una	revista	inglesa	*an*	*English*	*magazine*
	flor	interesante		*interesting*	*flower*
		blanca	*a*	*white*	
		roja		*red*	
		azul		*blue*	
	libros	ingleses		*English*	*books*
	periódicos	interesantes		*interesting*	*newspapers*
		blancos		*white*	
		rojos		*red*	
		azules		*blue*	
	revistas	inglesas		*English*	*magazines*
	flores	interesantes		*interesting*	*flowers*
		blancas		*white*	
		rojas		*red*	
		azules		*blue*	

4b

un	buen	libro		a	good	book
	gran	señor			great (big)	man
	pequeño	coche			small	car
una	buena	película		a	good	film
	gran	señora			great (big)	lady
	pequeña	flor			small	flower
	buenos	libros			good	books
	grandes	señores			great (big)	men
	pequeños	coches			small	cars
	buenas	películas			good	films
	grandes	señoras			great (big)	ladies
	pequeñas	flores			small	flowers

4c

El libro	es	bueno		The book	is	good
		barato				cheap
		español				Spanish
		grande				big
La película	es	buena, *etc.*		The film	is	
Los libros	son	buenos, *etc.*		The books	are	
Las películas	son	buenas, *etc.*		The films	are	

4d

¿ Es	interesante bueno, *etc.*	el libro? *etc.*		Is the book *etc.*	interesting? good?
¿ Es un	buen libro? libro interesante? *etc.*			Is it	a good book? an interesting book? *etc.*

5a

Me	gusta	el	té		I	like	tea
Nos			azúcar		We		sugar
		la	cerveza				beer
			leche				milk
	gustan	los	libros				books
			viajes				journeys
		las	películas				films
			mujeres				women

5b

No me	gusta gustan	el té los libros	*I don't like*	*tea* *books*
¿ Le	gusta gustan	el té? los libros?	*Do you like*	*tea?* *books?*
Sí,	me gusta me gusta el té		*Yes, I like*	*it* *tea*
¿ No le	gusta el té? gustan los libros?		*Don't you like*	*tea?* *books?*

EXPLANATIONS

1 The third person plural of verbs (what 'they' or 'you' plural [*Vds.*] are doing) ends in -*n*. E.g. *entra* he/she/it comes in
entran they come in.

2 Most Spanish adjectives follow the noun: e.g. *un adjetivo inglés* (an English adjective).

3 Some Spanish adjectives come before the noun, and certain of these have a shortened (apocopated) form. *Buen* is the shortened form of *bueno* and is used before the masculine noun (*un buen libro*). *Grande* is usually shortened to *gran* before a noun of either gender.

4 *Gustar* really means 'to please' as its use indicates: *me gusta* (it pleases me) is usually the equivalent of the English 'I like it'. *Me gusta el libro* (the book pleases me) is therefore 'I like the book'.

EXERCISES

1 En un bar hay dos españoles, Carlos y Pedro. Hablan mucho, beben cerveza, y fuman. También hay dos ingleses, Keith y John. Hablan poco, pero fuman mucho y beben vino. Los españoles hablan con los ingleses.

C. —¿ Les gustan los cigarrillos españoles?

J. —Sí, me gustan mucho. Vd. es muy amable.

K. —No me gustan los cigarrillos españoles, pero ¿quiere Vd. un cigarrillo inglés?

C. —Sí, por favor, me gustan mucho.

P. —¿ Vds. estudian el español?

J. —Sí, yo estudio el español, pero mi amigo no. Los libros españoles son muy interesantes.

19

1. ¿Hay ingleses en el bar?
2. Carlos, ¿es inglés?
3. ¿Quiénes hablan mucho?
4. ¿Quiénes hablan poco?
5. ¿Quiénes beben cerveza?
6. ¿Quiénes beben vino?
7. ¿Quién acepta un cigarrillo español?
8. ¿Quién no toma un cigarrillo español?
9. ¿Quién toma un cigarrillo inglés?
10. ¿Quién no estudia el español?

2 1. ¿Hay una tienda en el aeropuerto?
2. ¿Hay revistas españolas en la tienda?
3. ¿Hay películas?
4. ¿Qué mira la señorita?
5. ¿Quién toma leche?
6. ¿Toman refrescos en la tienda?
7. ¿Quiénes bajan?
8. ¿Las señoras bajan también?

3 You are in a shop in which you see a Spanish magazine, and you ask whether it is interesting. You want a book, and ask if a particular one is good. In the conversation which follows, tell the shopkeeper your nationality, that you like journeys, and that you like Spain. Then ask if there is a bar nearby, with English beer, and thank the shopkeeper for his help.

Give your side of the conversation, keeping strictly to expressions learnt so far.

Lección Cuatro

A Los ingleses están delante de la tienda.

B Los libros están en el mostrador.

C Los cigarrillos están en el paquete.

D El mozo está detrás del bar.

E Estoy en Londres.

F Estamos en la luna.

El español: ¿Dónde están el señor inglés y su mujer ahora?

El norteamericano: Allí están, delante de la tienda.

El español: Voy a comprar un periódico. Después, ¿quiere Vd. tomar un refresco conmigo?

El norteamericano: Sí, con mucho gusto.

El español (*al inglés y a su mujer*): ¿Quieren Vds. tomar un refresco con nosotros?

22

El inglés: Con mucho gusto.

    Entran en el bar.

El español: Vds. ¿qué van a tomar? ¿Café, vino, cerveza, naranjada?

La mujer del inglés: Una naranjada para mí, por favor.

El inglés: Para mí una cerveza, por favor.

El espanol: ¿Y para Vd.?

El norteamericano: Una copita de jerez, por favor. Me gusta beber el vino
    del país donde estoy.

El español: Vd. tiene razón. Como estamos en España, hay que beber vino
    español. ¡Mozo!

delante de – *in front of*	con nosotros – *with us*
la tienda – *shop*	la naranjada – *orange squash*
en – *on* (*see E2*)	para mí – *for me*
el mostrador – *counter*	la copita – *small glass*
detrás de – *behind*	el jerez – *sherry*
estoy – *I am* (*see E*1)	beber – *to drink*
la luna – *moon*	del país – *of the country*
ahora – *now*	Vd. tiene razón – *you are right*
allí – *there*	como – *as, since*
después – *afterwards*	hay que – *one must*
conmigo – *with me*	(*see FP3*)

FLUENCY PRACTICE

1

El señor / La señora	está	en	el	bar / aeropuerto	The	gentleman / lady	is	in	the	bar / airport
(El) (Ella) Vd.				puerto / comedor		He / She				port / dining-room
				café		You	are			café
Yo	estoy			hotel		I	am			hotel
Los señores / Las señoras	están		la	tienda / plaza	The	gentlemen / ladies	are			shop / square
(Ellos)				estación		They (*m*)				station
(Ellas) Vds.				América / España / Inglaterra		They (*f*) / You (*pl*) / We (*m*) / We (*f*)				South America / Spain / England
Nosotros / Nosotras	estamos									

23

2a

Está	en	la tienda	It's	in the shop
		el mostrador	He's	on the counter
			She's	

2b

Está	detrás	del	mostrador	It's	behind	the	counter
	delante		libro	He's	in front of		book
	debajo	de la	tienda	She's	under		shop
	cerca		mesa		near		table
	lejos	de los	mostradores		far away from		counters
	enfrente		libros		opposite		books
	al lado	de las	tiendas		beside		shops
	en el centro		mesas		in the middle of		tables

3

Quiero		hablar	I want	to	speak
Quiere		hablar español	It/he/she wants		speak Spanish
Vd. quiere		trabajar	You want(s)		work
Queremos		bajar	We want		come down
Quieren		cantar	They want		sing
Vds. quieren		bailar	You want (pl)		dance
Voy	a	mirar	I am going		look, watch
Va		escuchar	It/he/she is going		listen
Vd. va		estudiar	You (s) are going		study
Vamos		fumar	We are going		smoke
Van		pagar	They are going		pay
Vds. van		comprar algo	You (pl) are going		buy something
Me gusta		tomar algo	I like		take something
Le gusta (a Vd.)		hacer algo	He/she likes (You like)		do something
Nos gusta		estar en España	We like		be in Spain
Les gusta (a Vds.)		visitar el pueblo	They like (You like)		visit the town
Hay que		ayudar	I/you/she/he/we	must	help
		cruzar la calle	they/one/		cross the street
		pasar el puente			cross the bridge
		pasar una semana			spend a week here
		aquí			

NB With *gustar* the English could also be 'I like dancing' etc. but the Spanish does not change in this way.

EXPLANATIONS

1 *Ser* and *estar*. In this chapter the following forms of the verb 'to be' are practised:

está (he/she/it is).	We have already met: *es*
estoy (I am)	*soy*
están (they are)	*son*
estamos (we are)	*somos*

There are, as you can see, two forms of the verb 'to be' in Spanish, but they are not interchangeable. *Ser* is used to say what things are (*es un libro*—it's a book) and what their permanent qualities are (*es bueno*—it's good, *es español*—it's Spanish). *Estar* tells you where things are.

(Another use of *estar* is met in Chapter 6).

2 *En*. This has already been met, meaning 'in' and 'into'. In this chapter it also means 'on'. E.g. *en la tienda* (in the shop); *en el mostrador* (on the counter). Usually the context makes the meaning clear. When the Spanish is ambiguous, the meaning can be made clear by using *dentro de* to mean 'inside', and *sobre* (on), *encima de* (on top of, over).

3 *Debajo de, delante de, detrás de, dentro de*. These normally stand in front of *la, los,* or *las* but cannot stand in front of *el*, when the contracted form *del* must be used.

4 In Item 3 of the Fluency Practice, there is a long list of verbs ending in *-r* (*hablar*—to speak, etc.). This part of the verb is known as the infinitive and serves as a sort of name for the verb. E.g. in Note 1 (above) the different parts of the verb 'to be' are referred to by their infinitives *ser* and *estar*. You may have noticed that most of the verbs in the list end in *-ar* and, as many of them follow a common pattern, they form a group called '*-ar* verbs'. Similarly, *beber* and *comer* are '*-er*' verbs.

5 *Ellos* and *nosotros* are masculine, *ellas* and *nosotras* are feminine. A mixed group is always masculine.

6 *¿ Dónde . . .* ? and *Donde* (Where). The accent is used on the interrogative form.

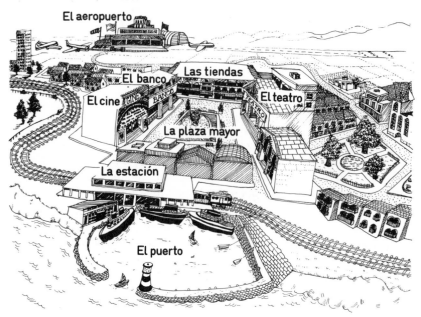

El aeropuerto

El banco   Las tiendas

El cine   CINE   BANCO   El teatro

La plaza mayor

La estación

El puerto

EXERCISES

1 1. ¿Está cerca de la estación el puerto?
   2. ¿Está cerca de la estación el aeropuerto?
   3. ¿Qué hay en la Plaza Mayor?
   4. ¿Qué hay enfrente de la estación?
   5. ¿Dónde está el cine?
   6. ¿Dónde está el banco?
   7. ¿Dónde están las tiendas?
   8. ¿Dónde están los aviones?

2 El señor Moffat está en España con la señora Moffat. Entran en un
  restaurante de la Avenida Generalísimo Franco. Quieren tomar refrescos.
  El mozo llega pronto con bocadillos, galletas, y café.
   1. ¿Quién está con el señor Moffat?
   2. ¿Dónde están?
   3. ¿Dónde entran?
   4. ¿Dónde está el restaurante?
   5. ¿Qué quieren tomar?
   6. ¿Les gusta el café?

7. ¿Esperan mucho?

8. ¿Dónde pone los refrescos el mozo?

9. ¿A Vd. le gusta esperar mucho en los restaurantes?

10. ¿Le gustan los bocadillos?

11. ¿Le gusta a Vd. estudiar el español?

12. ¿Le gusta a Vd. beber vino español?

13. ¿Está Vd. cerca de la estación?

14. ¿Le gusta a Vd. escuchar la radio?

15. ¿A Vd. le gusta trabajar mucho?

16. ¿Hay que esperar mucho en los aeropuertos?

3 Tell a Spaniard that you don't like smoking, but your wife does. She doesn't speak Spanish, but she wants to learn. She is going to look at the shops; she wants to buy something—and you are going to pay. You are both then going to have something in the bar, and going on to watch a French film.

If 'wife' doesn't meet the case, substitute 'husband', 'friend' etc. and make the appropriate changes.

Lección Cinco

A Toma un periódico . . .

B y lo lee.

C Abre una carta . . .

D y la lee.

E Saca caramelos . . .

F y los ofrece a Roberto.

G Ve unas corbatas . . .

H y las compra.

LA MAÑANA

—¿Quién es?

—Es el señor Martínez. Es muy puntual. Baja todos los días a las ocho. Bebe chocolate y come un huevo. Recibe muchas cartas; las abre y las lee. Entonces toma su periódico y lo lee.

—¿Y después?

—Sale a las nueve. Baja a la playa, anda, y mira el mar y los barcos. A las diez, mira su reloj de pulsera y sube a la terraza del Miramar. Toma café con leche.

—Luego, ¿mira su reloj de pulsera?

—Sí, lo mira siempre. A las once, va al café, y toma un helado. A mediodía, compra caramelos en el quiosco. Come y bebe mucho, ¿verdad?

—Sí, es verdad. ¿Los compra siempre allí?

—Sí, cada día va al quiosco.

—¿Y a la una?

—A la una, toma un aperitivo en el bar de Diego con unos amigos. Beben siempre vermut.

—Es puntualísimo este señor. No me gusta ser tan puntual.

—¿Por qué?

—Porque como cuando tengo hambre, bebo cuando tengo sed, y leo cuando quiero.

bebe – *he drinks* (*see E*1)
la mañana – *morning*
puntual – *punctual*
todos los días – *every day*
entonces – *then*
lo lee – *he reads it* (*see E*2)
sale (*from* salir) – *he goes out*
la playa – *beach*
anda (*from* andar) – *he walks*
el barco – *boat*
su – *his* (*see E*3)
luego – *then*
el reloj de pulsera – *wrist-watch*
sube (*from* subir) – *he goes up*
la terraza – *terrace*

siempre – *always*
un helado – *ice-cream*
mediodía – *midday*
¿verdad? – *doesn't he?* (*see E*6)
un aperitivo – *aperitif*
unos – *some* (*m.*)
vermut – *vermouth*
¿por qué? – *why?*
porque – *because*
cuando – *when*
tengo hambre – *I am hungry* (*see E*5)

29

FLUENCY PRACTICE

1

(no)	bebo	jerez vermut sidra			*I (don't)*	*drink*	*sherry* *vermouth* *cider*
	como	huevos pan naranjas				*eat*	*eggs* *bread* *oranges*
	recibo abro leo	periódicos cartas revistas				*receive* *open* *read*	*newspapers* *letters* *magazines*
	vivo	en	Londres Madrid Roma			*live*	*in*	*London* *Madrid* *Rome*

2a

Toma	un periódico unos periódicos una carta unas cartas	y	lo los la las	lee abre mira estudia

He takes	*a paper* *some papers* *a letter* *some letters*	*and*	*reads* *opens* *looks at* *studies*	*it* *them* *it* *them*

2b

Toma	un periódico unos periódicos una carta unas cartas	y quiere	leerlo abrirlos mirarla estudiarlas

He takes	*a paper* *some papers* *a letter* *some letters*	*and wants* *to*	*read it* *open them* *look at it* *study them*

3a

como	a	la una	*I eat*	*at*	*one o'clock*
subo	las	dos	*go upstairs*		*two*
leo		tres	*read*		*three*
escribo		cuatro	*write*		*four*
llego		cinco	*arrive*		*five*
toco el piano		seis	*play the piano*		*six*
saco una foto		siete	*take a snap*		*seven*
bailo		ocho	*dance*		*eight*
quiero salir		nueve	*want to go out*		*nine*
quiero comer		diez	*want to eat*		*ten*
hay un avión		once	*There's a plane*		*eleven*
hay un tren		doce	*There's a train*		*twelve*
		mediodía			*midday*
		medianoche			*midnight*

3b

¿Qué hora es?	Es la una	*What time is it?*	*It's one o'clock*
	Son las dos		*two o'clock*
	tres		*three*
	etc.		etc.

3c

¿A qué hora	come?	*What time*	*do you eat? have lunch?*
¿Cuándo	baila?	*When*	*do you dance?*
	cena?		*have dinner?*
	etc.		etc.

4

Es	mi	sombrero	*It's*	*my*	*hat*
		periódico			*newspaper*
		cuarto			*room*
		carta			*letter*
	su	amigo		*your*	*friend (m)*
		amiga		*his*	*friend (f)*
		novio		*her*	*boy-friend (fiancé)*
		novia			*girl-friend (fiancée)*
		lápiz			*pencil*
		novela			*novel*
Son	mis	sombreros	*They're*		*hats*
	sus	periódicos			*newspapers*
		etc.			etc.

5a

tengo	un libro	*I have*	*a book*
tiene	muchos amigos	*He has*	*many friends*
tienen	dos hermanas	*They have*	*two sisters*
	tres hermanos		*three brothers*
	poco dinero		*little money*

31

5b

tengo	hambre			I am	hungry
tiene	frío			He is	cold
tienen	sed			They are	thirsty
	calor				hot
	miedo				frightened
	razón				right
	sueño				sleepy

6

voy	al	bar	I am	going	to	the bar
va		café	He is			café
		norte	She			North
		sur	It			South
		oeste	You are			West
van		este	They			East
		Perú	You			Peru
		Japón				Japan
quiero ir	a la	terraza	I want to go			the terrace
tengo que ir		playa	I have to go			beach
subo		librería	I am going up			bookshop
sube		cárcel	He is going up			prison
suben	a	Francia	They are going up			France
		Bolivia				Bolivia

EXPLANATIONS

1 Three parts of the present tense of -er and -ir verbs are found here. They are regular verbs, i.e. they work to a regular pattern. The only differences here from -ar verbs is the 'e' in the third person singular and plural ending. In this chapter there are the -er verbs: beber, comer, leer, and the -ir verbs: recibir, abrir, vivir, salir and subir.

2 'It' is neuter in English but the Spanish object pronoun must be masculine or feminine, like the noun to which it refers. Lo (m. sing), la (f. sing) etc.

Notice the different place of the Spanish object pronoun, which comes before the verb (lo lee, he reads it) unless the verb is not finite (e.g. the infinitive leer in quiere leerlo, he wants to read it), when the object pronoun follows the verb and is written as part of it.

3 Mi, su. These possessive adjectives do not vary according to gender, but they vary according to the number of the noun to which they refer. E.g. mi amigo, mis amigos.

Su means 'his' or 'her', 'your' and 'their', singular.

Sus has these meanings when referring to more than one thing. If there is ambiguity, clarity can be achieved by the use of the noun followed by *de él* (his), *de ella* (hers), *de Vd.* (your), *de ellos* (their, m. or mixed), *de ellas* (their, f.) or *de Vds.* (your, pl.).E.g. *¿Es el abrigo de Vd.?* (Is it *your* coat?).

4 *Tengo, tiene* and *tienen* come from the verb *tener*. This is irregular, i.e. it does not work to the regular pattern for -er verbs, as will be seen from the first person singular *tengo*. In normal use *tener* means 'to have'.

5 *Tener hambre*, 'to be hungry' (lit. 'to have hunger'). Note that to be hungry, thirsty, sleepy, afraid, etc. are expressed by 'to have hunger, thirst,' etc.

6 *¿ Verdad?* A very common expression meaning 'is he?' 'doesn't it?' etc. *Verdad* means 'truth', so *¿ verdad?* can be used whenever one wants to say the equivalent of 'isn't that true?' The same as the French 'n'est ce pas?'

7 Just as we have *del* before a masculine noun and *de la* before a feminine noun, so we have *al* (to the— m.) and *a la* (to the—f.).

8 Most names of countries are feminine and are used without the article: *Inglaterra*, England, *a Inglaterra*, to England. But masculine names of countries always keep the *el*, combined with *a* or *de* as necessary: *el Perú, al Perú, del Perú*.

9 The irregular verb *ir* means 'to go'. The parts here are:

voy	I go	*van*	they or you (pl.) go
va	he/she/it goes		
	you go		

10 The ending -*ísimo* on *puntualísimo* means 'very, most, exceedingly'.

11 *¿ Cuándo?:* note the accent on the question form, as on *¿qué?* and *¿por qué?*

EXERCISES

1 1. ¿Vd. bebe mucho té?
2. ¿Le gusta a Vd. beber jerez?
3. ¿Come Vd. muchos huevos?
4. ¿Compra Vd. muchos periódicos?
5. ¿Recibe Vd. muchas cartas?
6. ¿Las abre con mucho gusto?
7. ¿Cuándo come Vd.?
8. ¿Vd. come a las tres de la mañana?

2 *Example:* Juan recibe una carta y la lee.
  Complete these sentences to this pattern:
  1. Compra una naranja y . . .
  2. Compra una botella de cerveza y . . .
  3. Recibe unos libros y . . .
  4. Les gustan los huevos: . . . con mucho gusto.
  5. Saca unos caramelos y . . .
  6. Aprende el inglés: . . . muy bien.
  7. Compra unas revistas pero no . . .
  8. Toma un vaso de leche pero no . . .

3 1. Quiero tomar el tren. Voy a la estación.
  2. Quiero tomar el avión.   . . .
  3. Tengo hambre.   . . .
  4. Tengo sed.   . . .
  5. Quiero comprar un libro.   . . .
  6. Quiero mirar una película.   . . .
  7. Quiero dinero.   . . .
  8. Me gusta mirar los barcos.   . . .

4 Translate: (See F.P.4 and E.3)
  1. Your sandwich is going to come soon.
  2. Your coffee is on the table.
  3. The waiter is coming with my tea.
  4. My bedroom is very small.
  5. Is your bedroom big or small?
  6. Pedro is just arriving with his wife.
  7. Her hat is very big.
  8. Their car is French.

A Mira el libro.

B Mira a Roberto.

C Mata una mosca.

D Mata a un hombre.

E Mira el pasaporte.

F Mira a la chica.

EN LA LIBRERÍA

Ian:	Bueno, ¿qué vamos a hacer hoy?
Jaime:	¿Qué día es?
Ian:	Es martes.
Jaime:	Pues hay que esperar a Roberto. Es muy perezoso. A las diez vamos a la librería.
Ian:	¿Vds. leen mucho?
Jaime:	Sí, leemos muchísimos libros. Estudiamos literatura española —novelas, poesía, teatro. Bueno, vuelve Roberto. Ya podemos ir.

(*Pronto llegan a la librería*)

Ian:	¿Qué piensa Vd. de esta novela?
El librero:	Es muy buena. El autor cuenta su niñez en España, y describe sus viajes por toda América, donde mata a un hombre. Es interesante, pero no es difícil.
Ian:	Gracias, la tomo. Mi mujer pide un libro de poesía. ¿Puede Vd. recomendar algo?
El librero:	Sí, hay una pequeña antología bastante fácil. Aquí está. La novela cuesta ciento veinte pesetas y la antología ciento diez. Son doscientas treinta pesetas en todo, señor. Muchas gracias, señor.

la librería – *bookshop*
hoy – *today*
martes – *Tuesday*
　　(*see FP2b and E*)
esperar – *to wait for*
perezoso – *lazy*
a las diez – *at ten o'clock*
la literatura – *literature*
una novela – *novel*
la poesía – *poetry*
el teatro – *theatre*
vuelve – *returns*
　　(*from* volver) (*see FP2a and E3*)
pronto – *soon, quickly*
¿que piensa Vd? – *what do you*
　　(*from* pensar)　*think?*

cuenta – *tells*
　　(*from* contar) (*see FP2a*)
niñez – *childhood*
un viaje – *journey*
difícil – *difficult*
pide (*from* pedir) – *she asks for*
　　(*see E8*)
una antología – *anthology*
bastante – *enough*
fácil – *easy*
cuesta – *costs*
　　(*from* costar)
doscientas treinta – *two hundred and thirty*
en todo – *in all*

FLUENCY PRACTICE

1

				We		John
miramos	a	Juan		We	are looking at	John
esperamos		Paloma			waiting for	Paloma
queremos		la misma chica			in love with	the same girl
saludamos		los	demás		greet	others
conocemos			otros		know	others (m)
recibimos		las	otras		receive	others (f)
	al	Señor Tellez				Señor Tellez
		General				the General

(no)	somos	turistas	We are	(not)	tourists
		ingleses			English
		perezosos			lazy
		músicos			musicians
		idiotas			idiots
		los hermanos de Jaime			Jaime's brothers

(no)	estamos	cansados	We are	(not)	tired
		muy satisfechos			very satisfied
		aquí			here
		cerca del pueblo			near the town
		lejos de la playa			far from the beach
		demasiado lejos			too far away

(no)	tenemos	mucho dinero		We have	(not)	much money	
		bastante	dinero			enough	money
			tiempo				time
		hambre		We are	(not)	hungry	
		frío				cold	

(no)	vamos	al	baile	We are	(not) going	to the	dance
			banco				bank
		a la	estación				station
			taberna				inn
		hacia el norte					towards the north
		lejos de aquí					far from here
		a bailar					to dance

2a

pienso	que es	muy interesante	I think	(that) it is	very interesting
piensa		tarde	He thinks		late
pensamos	en	nuestra madre	We think	about	our mother
piensan		su país	They think		their country

2b

cuento	historias ridículas	I am	telling	silly stories
cuenta	su vida	He is		his life story
contamos	el dinero	We are	counting	the money
cuentan	los platos	They are		the dishes
	con Jaime			on Jaime

vuelvo	a las tres	I am	coming back	at three o'clock
vuelve	a España	He* is	going back	to Spain
volvemos	con Elena	We are		with Elena
vuelven	por tren	They are		by train

* she, it; you are

2c

puedo	ir mañana		I	can	go tomorrow
puede	volver el	lunes	He	come back on	Monday
		martes	She		Tuesday
		miércoles	It		Wednesday
		jueves	You		Thursday
podemos		viernes	We		Friday
pueden		sábado	They		Saturday
		domingo	You		Sunday
	comprar cigarrillos aquí				buy cigarettes here
	andar muy de prisa				walk very fast
	descansar un rato				rest for a while

3a

(no)	conozco	a Elena	I	(don't)	know	Elena
	conoce	al Señor Torres	He	(doesn't)		Señor Torres
	conocemos	al librero	We	(don't)		the bookseller
	conocen	a la cantante	They			singer (f)
		el pueblo				town
		un lugar interesante				an interesting place

3b

(no)	sé	tocar	el piano	I	(don't)	know	how to	play the piano
	sabe		la guitarra	He	(doesn't)			guitar
	sabemos	hablar chino		We	(don't)			speak Chinese
	saben	que es muy interesante		They	(don't)			that it is very interesting
		donde está						where it is
		muchas cosas						many things
		por qué no quiere bajar						why he doesn't want to come down

EXPLANATIONS

1 a) Personal '*a*'. When a specified person is the object of a verb in Spanish, the personal *a* must be used. *Mira el libro* (he looks at the book); but *mira a Pedro* (he looks at Pedro), *mira al hombre* (he looks at the man). This can be extended to animals when they are being considered as near-humans.

1 b) First person plural of verbs: in regular verbs, the infinitive ending is replaced by -*amos* for -*ar* verbs, -*emos* for -*er* verbs, and -*imos* for -*ir* verbs. E.g. *bailamos* (we dance), *esperamos* (we wait), *bebemos* (we drink), *comemos* (we eat), *recibimos* (we receive), *vivimos* (we live). The forms for the irregular verbs so far met are:

ser: *somos*, we are
estar: *estamos*, we are
tener: *tenemos*, we have
ir: *vamos*, we go

If a subject pronoun is needed, it is *nosotros* (we) m. or mixed, *nosotras* (we) f.

2 *Ser* and *estar*. It was mentioned earlier that *ser* is used with permanent qualities; for temporary conditions, *estar* must be used. Hence *somos perezosos* (we are lazy) would indicate fundamental laziness; as tiredness is temporary we say *estamos cansados* (we are tired). To use the wrong verb is either totally incorrect or changes the meaning completely: e.g. *es cansado* does not mean 'he is tired' but 'he is tiring' i.e. a bore.

3 *Pensar* (to think), *contar* (to relate, count), *volver* (to return), *pedir* (to ask for) and *costar* (to cost) are almost regular verbs of a type very common in Spanish. Removing the infinitive ending (-*ar*, -*er*, -*ir*) leaves the stem (also called the root or radical). The stem in these verbs changes when it is stressed, so we obtain the radicals *piens-*, *cuent-*, *vuelv-*, *pid-*, *cuest-*, to which the singular endings and third person plural ending (-*o*, -*a*, -*e*, or -*an*, -*en*) are added. The first person plural ending, -*amos*, -*emos*, -*imos*, receives the stress under the usual rules for stressing, so here the radical does not change. These verbs are called radical-changing verbs.

4 *Poder* (to be able) is an irregular verb, but is a straightforward radical-changing verb in its present tense: *puedo*, *puede*, *podemos*, *pueden*.

5 *Poder* and *saber*. *Poder* is used when the subject is physically capable of doing what follows; *saber* (to know) has the meaning of being able to do something which requires special skill. *No puede hablar*, 'he can't speak' (because of impediment or strangulation); *no sabe hablar* 'he can't

speak'; (probably because he is too young) *no sabe hablar español* 'he can't speak Spanish' (because he hasn't learned it).

6 *Saber* and *conocer*. *Saber* is to know a fact; *conocer* is to know someone or be acquainted with something. *Sabe que el pueblo está cerca* 'he knows that the town is near'; *conoce el pueblo* 'he knows the town'.

7 Days of the week only have a capital letter when they start a sentence. There is no need for an equivalent of 'on' in English sentences like 'he is coming on Monday' (*viene el lunes*); 'every Monday' (*los lunes*).
For a full list of the days of the week see FP 2(b).

8 *Pedir a* is to ask someone for something, so 'I ask him for a stamp' is *le pido un sello*; i.e. the English word 'for' is not expressed by an equivalent Spanish word.

EXERCISES

1 El señor y la señora Roberts son turistas ingleses. Tienen un gran cuarto en el hotel Sánchez. Les gusta mucho el hotel y les gusta España.

El hotel está cerca de la playa. Pueden ver el mar. A las diez, bajan y andan en la playa. Compran muchas cosas en las tiendas y vuelven al hotel a la una de la tarde.

(*They meet a Spanish couple.*)

—¿Vds. son franceses?

—No, somos turistas ingleses.

Continue the conversation. You may wish to go beyond one o'clock and say what they do in the afternoon.

2 Translate:

Mary is a waitress. She is in the hotel. She is giving refreshments to the men. They are thirsty and tired, and they are telling stupid stories. They are very boring but they think they are very interesting. They are going back to Madrid on Wednesday.

3 Ken can speak Spanish. He knows many Spaniards and can play the guitar very well. With his friends he can go to many Spanish towns. They know many interesting things.

4 A ¿Qué hace la chica?   B ¿Qué hace el señor?

C ¿Qué hace el señor?   D ¿Qué hace el muchacho?

A Paloma está en su casa. Pasa Jaime.

B Le da una rosa.

C Jaime coge su mano

D y le da un beso.

E Los niños lloran.

F Jaime les da caramelos.

EL CUMPLEAÑOS DE ROBERTO

Jaime: Hoy es el cinco de abril: es el cumpleaños de Roberto. ¿Qué puedo darle?

Isabel: ¿Por qué no le ofrece una corbata? Le gustan las corbatas.

Jaime: Bueno, le regalo una corbata. ¿Esta corbata le parece bien?

Ian: No, no me gusta, pero aquella corbata me gusta mucho.

42

Jaime:	Bueno, la tomo. Es bastante cara, pero es de seda. Además, cuando es mi cumpleaños Roberto me da siempre una corbata. Ahora, ¿les falta algo a Vds.?
Isabel:	Sí, nos falta una película y postales para nuestros amigos.
Jaime:	Podemos comprarlas aquí también. Y me faltan sobres: tengo que escribir muchas cartas.
Isabel:	¿A todas sus amigas?
Jaime:	Ellas me escriben mucho, y tengo que responderles, claro.
Ian:	¿Y escribe también a Paloma?
Jaime:	A Paloma no, pero voy a mandarle flores.

está en su casa – *is at home*
coge (*from* coger) – *he takes*
le da un beso – *he kisses it*
llorar – *to cry*
caramelos – *sweets*
el cinco de abril – *5th April*
(*see E7 and 8*)
el cumpleaños – *birthday*
¿qué puedo darle? – *What can I give him?*
(*see E2*)
le regalo – *I'll give him*
(*see E1*)
parecer – *to appear*
¿le parece bien? – *does it look good to you?*

aquella corbata – *that tie*
la tomo – *I'll have it*
(*see E3*)
bastante caro – *quite dear*
la seda – *silk (see E9)*
ahora – *now*
¿les falta algo a Vds.? – *do you need anything else?*
(*see E4*)
una postal – *a post-card*
un sobre – *an envelope*
tengo que – *I must*
responder – *to reply*
mandar – *to send*
flores – *flowers*

FLUENCY PRACTICE

1

Roberto	ve	a	Carmen	y le	da	una rosa
	encuentra		Lolita		ofrece	caramelos
	quiere		Maite		manda	una pulsera

Roberto	*sees*	*Carmen*	*and*	*gives*	*her*	*a rose*
	meets	*Lolita*		*offers*		*sweets*
	loves	*Maite*		*sends*		*a bracelet*

43

2

Jaime	encuentra ve llama	a al al	Roberto Isabel mozo empleado	y le pide	un cigarrillo sus señas una cerveza informaciones

	Jaime	meets sees calls	Roberto Isabel the waiter clerk	and asks	him her	for	a cigarette his/her address a beer information

3

Siempre Nunca	me le nos les	da manda regala ofrece	un libro una postal dinero un bolígrafo
		deja	su periódico joyas
		escribe	una carta

He*	always never	gives sends gives offers	me him† us them	a book a postcard money a ballpoint
		leaves		his/ her paper jewels
		writes		a letter

* she, it, you give † her

4

Quiero Tengo que	decirle algo darle esta carta	(?)
¿ Puedo	ofrecerle algo pedirles noticias darle algo típico	

I want to have	tell you* something give you this letter	(?)
May I	offer you something ask you for news give you something typical	

* him, her

5

(no)	va van	a	mandarme ofrecernos pedirnos darles	un paquete caramelos dinero unos relojes de oro corbatas de seda
	quiere quieren		hablarme respondernos escribirle	cada mes

He She You They	is are	(not) going to	send me offer us ask us for give them	a parcel sweets money gold watches silk ties
He She You They	wants want	to	speak to me answer us write to him	every month

6

Me	mira	He	looks* at	me
le	ve	She	sees	him
la	busca		looks for	her
lo	halla		finds	it
nos	conoce		knows	us
les	deja		leaves	them (m)(persons)
las	quiere		wants/loves	them (f)(objects
los	escucha		listens to	or persons)
			* or you look, etc.	them (m)(objects)

7

Quiere	mirarme	He	wants* to	look at me
Puede	verle	She	can	see him
Va a	buscarla		is going to	look for her
	hallarla			find her
	conocernos			get to know us
	dejarles			leave them (m)(persons)
	escucharlos			listen to them (m)(objects)

* or *you want, are going to*

8

Me	falta	dinero	I	need	money
Le		sentido común	you	lack	commonsense
		un lápiz	he	needs	a pencil
		gasolina	she	needs	petrol
nos	faltan	sobres	we	need	envelopes
les		noticias	you		news
		sellos	they		stamps
Me	gusta	la paella	I	like	paella
Le		el vino	you*		wine
nos	gustan	los calamares	we		squid
les		los helados	they		ice cream

* or *he/she likes*

9

Este	bolígrafo	es	mío	This	ballpoint	is	mine
esta	novela		nuestra		novel		ours
ese	periódico		nuestro	That	paper		ours
esa	corbata		mía		tie		mine
aquel	lápiz		suyo		pencil		his*
aquella	carta		suya		letter		his*
estos	bolígrafos	son	míos	These	ballpoints	are	mine
estas	novelas		mías		novels		mine
esos	periódicos		nuestros	Those	papers		ours
esas	corbatas		nuestras		ties		ours
aquellos	lápices		suyos		pencils		his*
aquellas	cartas		suyas		letters		his*

*hers, yours, theirs, also.

El primero de enero es el día de año nuevo.
El veinticinco de diciembre es el día de Navidad.
El tres de abril es el cumpleaños de Paloma.
Salgo de aquí el catorce de agosto.
Jaime llega el siete de marzo.
La tienda está cerrada desde el cuatro hasta el veinte.

> *The first of January is New Year's Day.*
> *The twenty-fifth of December is Christmas Day.*
> *The third of April is Paloma's birthday.*
> *I leave here on the fourteenth of August.*
> *James arrives on the seventh of March.*
> *The shop is closed from the fourth to the twentieth.*

11

Busco	la corbata de	Roberto	*I'm looking for*	*Robert's tie*	
No hallo	las señas de del de	Maite hotel la taberna	*I can't find*	*Maite's address* *the address of the*	*hotel* *inn*
es	la mesa de	los ingleses las francesas	*It is*	*the English people's* *the French*	*table*
	el coche de	sus amigos aquellos amigos suyos		*Your friends' car* *the car of those friends* *of yours*	

EXPLANATIONS

1 The indirect object pronouns are the same as the direct object pronouns except for *le* (to him, to her, to it, to you) and *les* (to them, to you [pl.]).

In English there are two structures, 'I give him the book' and 'I give the book to him'. It helps to think only of the second one, which shows the indirect object by the word 'to'. The only possible Spanish is *le doy el libro*.

2 Like direct object pronouns, the indirect object pronouns follow the infinitive and are written as part of it: *quiero decirle* algo (I want to say something to you/him/her).

3 When the direct object is a person, *le* stands for 'him', *la* stands for 'her', *les* for 'them' (masc. or mixed) and *las* for 'them' (f.). Thus *le veo* 'I see him, or you' (m.); *la veo* 'I see her, or you' (f.). (In some areas of Spain, *lo* is used for persons instead of *le* and in some others *le* is used for things instead of *lo*, but the above is the accepted usage).

4 *Faltar* is like *gustar*: so 'I need, lack, am short of . . .' is *me falta*.

5 *Este* means 'this . . . (near me)', *ese*—'that . . . (near you)', *aquél*—'that . . . (away from both of us)'. *Ése* can mean 'that . . . of yours (his, etc.)' and can be pejorative.

6 *Mío*—'mine', and like other forms listed in Fluency Practice 9, agrees with its noun.

7 Dates: the first of the month is the ordinal *primero*; but the cardinal numbers are used for all the other dates. As with days, 'on the third' is simply *el tres*.

8 Names of months (listed Chapter 12, FP 2) are not written with a capital.

9 *La corbata de Roberto* has the same structure as 'the tie of Robert', not the usually employed English form 'Robert's tie'. It is the only way of expressing the possessive. The same construction is used for *una corbata de seda*—a silk tie (lit. 'a tie of silk').

EXERCISES

1 *Example:* Carlos tiene hambre. Luis le da un bocadillo.
  1. Jaime tiene sed.   . . .
  2. Antonio quiere fumar.   . . .
  3. A Maite le gustan las flores.   . . .
  4. Pepe quiere escribir a Isabel.   . . .
  5. A Jorge le gusta leer.   . . .
  6. La señora Cummins y su marido quieren tomar refrescos.   . . .
  7. Unas chicas lloran.   . . .

2 *Example:* ¿Está aquí el señor Ayala? —Sí, Vd. puede verle.
  1. Los músicos llegan. Vamos a   . . .
  2. ¿Quiere Vd. recibir al señor Cummins! —Sí, puedo   . . .
  3. Juan busca a Herminio. No   . . .
  4. Maite no conoce a Pablo. Quiere   . . .
  5. ¿Dónde están los ingleses? Tengo que   . . .

3 After sharing a room with someone for some time, your belongings have got mixed up: worse than that, someone else's property seems to be there too. Sort out this problem in Spanish.

4 Write out in Spanish:

    1. John's birthday is on the twenty-seventh of July.

    2. New Year's Day is the first of January.

    3. Helen's car will be here on the fourth of May.

    4. The Italian girl's friend is arriving on the fourteenth of August.

    5. Paco's bar is closed from the twelfth to the twenty-second.

    6. He doesn't work on the first of May.

Lección Ocho

A Hace sol.

B Hace calor.

C Está bebiendo.

D Bebe mucho.

E Está fumando.

F Fuma mucho.

Ian: Buenos días. Como ayer está leyendo el periódico.

Jaime: ¡Claro está! Como ayer, estoy esperando a Roberto. Siempre llega tarde. Es muy perezoso. Nunca se levanta antes de las ocho. Y se hace cada día más perezoso.

Roberto: ¡Ay, qué mentiras! Ya estoy aquí. Me levanto siempre a las siete y media, antes que tú.

49

Jaime:	Te digo que tú no te levantas nunca antes de las ocho. Doña Elena, son ya las nueve y cuarto, ¿no? Claro, Roberto, como tú nunca te acuestas antes de las tres, siempre estás cansado. Bueno, vámonos.
Roberto:	Pero tengo que tomar algo antes de salir.
Jaime:	Bueno, hombre, siéntate y desayúnate. Pero tienes que darte prisa. Doña Elena e Ian te están esperando. Toma tu café.
Ian:	Pues no tenemos prisa. Estamos disfrutando del sol, del calor . . .
Jaime:	¡Cuidado! Se están poniendo como Roberto.

hace sol – *it is sunny*
    (*see E12*)
hace calor – *it is hot*
como – *like*
ayer – *yesterday*
tarde – *late*
se hace – *he is getting*
    (*see E1*)
se levanta – *he gets up*
    (*see E3*)
antes – *before*
¡ay! – *cry of pain, anguish or protest*
e = y *before 'i' or 'hi'*
una mentira – *a lie*

ya – *already*
digo – *I say*
nunca – *never*
te acuestas – *you go to bed*
    (*see FP2a*)
vámonos – *let's go*
siéntate – *sit down!*
    (*see FP6c*)
desayunarse – *to have breakfast*
darse prisa – *to hurry up*
pues – *but*
tener prisa – *to be in a hurry*
disfrutar de algo – *to enjoy something*
¡cuidado! – *careful!*
ponerse – *to become*

FLUENCY PRACTICE

1a

aquí	siempre	hace	sol
allí	nunca		viento
en el norte	casi siempre		frío
en España	casi nunca		mucho viento
en nuestro país	normalmente	está lloviendo	
		nieva	

Here	*it is*	*always*	*sunny*
there		*never*	*windy*
in the North		*nearly always*	*cold*
in Spain		*almost never*	*very windy*
in our country		*usually*	*raining*
			snowing

50

1b

llueve	mucho	it rains	a lot
	poco		very little

hay mucha nieve		there is a lot of snow

2a

me	levanto	a	las ocho			I	get up	at	8
	acuesto		las once				go to bed		11
	duermo		la una de la noche				go to sleep		1 a.m.
te	levantas		las tres de la mañana			You	get up		3 a.m.
	acuestas		las siete de la tarde				go to bed		7 p.m.
	duermes		las siete	y	cinco		go to sleep		7.5
se	levanta				diez	He/	gets up		7.10
	acuesta				cuarto*	She	goes to bed		7.15
	duerme				veinte		goes to sleep		7.20
nos	levantamos				veinticinco	We	get up		7.25
	acostamos				media*		go to bed		7.30
	dormimos		las ocho	menos	veinticinco		go to sleep		7.35
se	levantan				veinte	They	get up		7.40
	acuestan				cuarto*		go to bed		7.45
	duermen				diez		go to sleep		7.50
					cinco				7.55
			en punto					exactly 8 o'clock	
			eso de las nueve					about nine	
			diez					ten	

*y cuarto, *quarter past;* y media, *half-past;* menos cuarto, *quarter to.*

2b

quiero levantarme	antes de	medianoche	I	want	to get up	before	midnight
quieres levantarte	después de	la una	You	want		after	one
quiere levantarse		las cinco	He*	wants			five
queremos levantarnos	antes que	tú	We	want			you
quieren levantarse		él	They	want			him
		Roberto					Roberto
	después de	todo el mundo					everybody
	cuando	quiero				when	I	like
		quieres					you	like
		quiere					he	likes
		queremos					we	like
		quieren					they	like
	temprano					early	
	tarde					late	

* or *she*

3

¿Cómo	te llamas? se llama? llaman?					*What*	*are* *is* *are*	*you* *he** *they**	*called?*

Me llamo se llama	Jaime Martínez					*I* *he**	*am* *is*	*called*	*Jaime* *Martínez*
	una blusa coñac					*it*			*a blouse* *brandy*
se llaman	faldas zapatos calcetines cordones					*they*	*are*		*skirts* *shoes* *socks* *laces*

4   ** she, you*

Se	lava		la cara las manos los dientes			*He** *She **	*washes* *cleans*	*his/her*	*face* *hands* *teeth*
	peina		(el pelo)				*combs*		*hair*
	afeita						*shaves*		
	hace mal						*hurts*	*himself/ herself*	
		en	la	rodilla pierna cabeza				*his*	*knee* *leg* *head*
			el	pie brazo					*foot* *arm*

*You wash your face, etc.

5a

Todo el día Este mes	está	escuchando la radio cantando		
Esta semana Este año	estoy	visitando a	su mi	familia abuelo novia
	estamos	disfrutando	del	calor sol
			de la	música

He is	*listening to the radio* *singing*			*all day long* *this month*
I am	*visiting*	*his* *my*	*family* *grandfather* *girl-friend*	*this week* *this year*
We are	*enjoying*	*the*	*heat* *sun* *music*	

5b

se está	poniendo	de más en más	perezoso (-a)
			alegre
			estúpido (-a)
			aburrido (-a)
			guapo (-a)

He is	*getting*	*lazier and lazier*	
She		*happier and happier*	
You are		*more and more*	*stupid*
			boring
		prettier and prettier	

6a

(No)	tome (Vd.)	una manzana	(*Don't*)	*take*	*an apple*
	mire	aquel señor		*look at*	*that gentleman*
	abra	esta carta		*open*	*this letter*
	venga	por aquí		*come*	*this way*
	siga	este camino		*follow*	*this road*
	toma				
	mira				
	abre				
	ve				
	sigue				
	tomen (Vds.)				
	miren				
6b	*etc.*				

tómela (Vd.) (*polite*)	*take it* (*f*)
mírele	*look at him*
ábrala	*open it* (*f*)
sígalo	*follow it* (*m*)

tómala (*familiar*)
mírale
ábrela
síguelo

tómenla (Vds.) (*polite pl.*)
mírenle
   etc.

6c

siéntese	*sit down*
levántese	*stand up*
siéntense	*sit down* (*pl*)
levántense	*stand up* (*pl*)

no se	siente	*don't*	*sit down*
	levante		*stand up*
	sienten		*sit down* (*pl*)
	levanten		*stand up* (*pl*)

53

no	la tome	*don't*	*take*	*it(f)*
	le mire		*look at*	*her, him*
	la abra		*open*	*it(f)*
	lo siga		*follow*	*it(m)*

EXPLANATIONS

1 *Hacer* (to do, to make): an irregular verb. Present tense *hago, haces, hace, hacemos, hacen. Se hace*, 'he/she/it is becoming'.

2 *Hacer* is used idiomatically in weather expressions: e.g. *hace sol* 'it is sunny'.

3 Reflexive verbs. Verbs like *se levanta, me acuesto* are called reflexive because the action of the verb reflects back to the subject. *Se levanta* literally means 'he raises himself', *me acuesto* 'I lay myself down'. The reflexive pronouns *me, te, se, nos* cannot be omitted. The infinitive has -*se* added to it to show that it is reflexive: *levantarse, acostarse,* (the latter radical changing).

When the infinitive depends upon another verb, the reflexive pronoun matches the subject of that verb: *quiero acostarme* 'I want to go to bed'; *quiere acostarse* 'he wants to go to bed'; *queremos acostarnos* 'we want to go to bed'. In these cases no stress mark is needed, but it is necessary in the imperative form (see no. 8).

4 *Tú*. This is the familiar form for 'you'. It is used within the family and between close friends, and fairly widely where *Vd.* would be felt to be too formal. The visitor to Spain should use it only when invited to do so, except to very young children and pets.

It takes the second person singular form of the verb, which ends in -*s* (*fumas, comes, escribes, eres* (from *ser*), *estás* (from *estar*), *tienes, vuelves, vas*).

5 The familiar possessive adjective is *tu* s., *tus* pl. *Tu camisa* 'your shirt'.

6 With reflexive verbs and parts of one's body, no possessive is needed: *me lavo la cara, se lava la cara*. With the verb *doler* (to hurt, ache) 'my head aches' is *me duele la cabeza*.

Even when the subject of the verb and its object are different people, the meaning is clear: *le lava el brazo* 'he washes his arm' (someone else's because if it were his own it would be *se lava el brazo*).

7 Although the ordinary present tense of Spanish verbs is expressed in English either by the simple present or the present continuous (pro-

gressive form) e.g. *baila* 'she dances', 'she is dancing', there is a parallel to the continuous form: *está bailando*. It is formed from the present tense of *estar* and the gerund (present participle) of the action verb. The gerund is formed by removing the infinitive ending from regular verbs and adding *-ando* for *-ar* verbs: *fumando* (smoking), and *-iendo* for *-er* and *-ir* verbs: *comiendo* (eating) and *recibiendo* (receiving). Irregular verbs have these endings, but the stems are often irregular:

ser:	*siendo*	*hacer:*	*haciendo*
estar:	*estando*	*poder:*	*pudiendo*
tener:	*teniendo*	*dormir:*	*durmiendo*
ir:	*yendo*		

8 The imperative form of the verb is used for commands. The second person singular (*tú*) form simply drops its final *-s* in regular verbs. The polite (*Vd.*) form is really the subjunctive: for regular verbs, use the endings *-e*, *-en* with *-ar* verbs, and *-a*, *-an* with *-er* and *-ir* verbs.

When used with reflexive verbs, the addition of the reflexive pronoun immediately after the imperative would displace the stress, so this is restored to its correct place by use of the stress mark. *Se levanta Vd.* 'you are getting up' (stress on second syllable): *levántese Vd.* 'get up'.

The same process takes place when an object pronoun is added to the imperative *ábrela* 'open it' (f); *hágalo* 'do it'.

The imperative can easily sound rude, so it is wise to add *por favor*.

9 *Seguir.* A radical-changing verb with minor spelling complications. The hard *g* is to be preserved, so *gu* is needed before *-e*, *-i* but not before the other vowels; present tense: *sigo, sigues, sigue, seguimos, siguen.* Gerund: *siguiendo.*

EXERCISES

1 1. ¿A qué hora se levanta Vd.?
   2. ¿A qué hora se desayuna?
   3. ¿A qué hora sale de casa? —Salgo ...
   4. ¿A qué hora cena Vd.?
   5. ¿A qué hora se acuesta?

2 Invite (a) a close friend, (b) a stranger, (c) several strangers to:
   1. speak
   2. come in
   3. come down

4. sing
5. listen
6. drink more beer
7. eat something else.
8. read some magazines

3 It is raining heavily, although it is still very hot. You are listening to the radio: the programme is very interesting. Somebody telephones you from a nearby town to invite you to a dance. You are tired and intend to go to bed early, so you make some excuses but eventually have to give in and promise to go later. Using expressions from all parts of the course so far, give your side of the conversation, or both.

Lección Nueve

A Él es más grande que ella.
B España es más grande que Inglaterra.

C Jorge es el mejor guitarrista.
D El caballo de Ricardo es el peor.

Roberto: Dígame señor, ¿cuándo hay un tren para Barcelona?

Empleado: Acaba de salir uno, señor. El próximo llega a las diez menos cuarto, y sale a las diez en punto.

Roberto: ¿Y a qué hora llega a Barcelona?

Empleado: Llega a las once y veinte señor.

Roberto: ¿Se para mucho?

Empleado: No, señor, se para en sólo tres estaciones.

Roberto: Bueno, pues, tomo tres billetes.

Empleado: ¿Qué clase, señor?

Roberto: Primera, por favor.

Empleado: ¿Quiere Vd. billetes sencillos?

Roberto: No, señor, ida y vuelta, por favor.

Elena: Oh, el andén es más bajo que en Inglaterra. Los trenes son más grandes.

Ian: Sí, o parecen serlo. Hay que hacer un esfuerzo para subir.

Roberto: Póngase aquí, cerca de la ventanilla. Este es el mejor sitio; se ve muy bien. El viaje es muy interesante, con vistas espléndidas. Y Vd. puede sacar fotos.

el mejor – *the best* (*see E2*)
el peor – *the worst*
el empleado – *employee*
dígame – *tell me*
(*from* decir) (*see FP5*)
acaba de salir – *it has just left*
(*see E5 and FP4*)
el próximo – *the next one*
en punto – *exactly*
pararse – *to stop*
sólo – *only*
pues – *then*
el billete – *ticket*

primera clase – *first class*
sencillo – *single*
ida y vuelta – *return*
bajo – *low*
parecen serlo – *they seem to be*
un esfuerzo – *effort*
póngase – *sit* (*lit. place yourself*) (*see E6*)
la ventanilla – *window* (*of vehicle*)
un sitio – *place*
una vista – *view*
espléndido(-a) – *splendid*

La taquilla
BILLETES
El locomotivo
El vagón
El andén
El mozo
La maleta
El jefe de estación
Los viajeros   LA ESTACIÓN

FLUENCY PRACTICE

1a

Jaime	es	más	alto (-a)	que	Roberto
Jorge		menos	delgado (-a)		Luis
Paloma			gordo (-a)		Maite
Carmen			pequeño (-a)		Dolores
			rico (-a)		yo
			guapo (-a)		tú
			inteligente		nosotros
Este libro		mejor			aquél
Esta película		peor			aquélla
					el mío
					la suya

Jaime	*is*	*taller*		*than*	*Roberto*
Jorge		*slimmer*			*Luis*
Paloma		*fatter*			*Maite*
Carmen		*smaller*			*Dolores*
		richer			*I*
		more	*handsome/pretty*		*you*
			intelligent		*us*
		less	*tall*		
			slim		
			fat		
			small		
			rich		
This book		*better*			*that one* (*m*)
This film		*worse*			*that one* (*f*)
					mine
					yours

NB As, by this stage, the rules for choice of masculine and feminine adjectives will have been fully grasped, together with the meanings of much of the vocabulary, strict correspondence between the Spanish and English tables has not been adhered to, in the interest of brevity.

1b

Los	franceses	son	más	lógicos	que	los	ingleses
	norteamericanos			ricos			europeos
Las	naranjas de Sevilla		mejores			las	de Brighton

The	*French*	*are*	*more logical*		*than*	*the*	*English*
	Americans		*richer*				*Europeans*
Seville oranges			*better*				*Brighton ones*

2a

Jaime Jorge	es	el	más	alto rico	de	todos	Jaime Jorge	is the	tallest richest	of all
Paloma Carmen		la		guapa inteligente		todas	Paloma Carmen		prettiest cleverest	
Este libro		el mejor				todos	This book		best	

2b

Jaime y Paloma	son	los más corteses	de	todos
Los franceses norteamericanos		lógicos ricos		
Las naranjas de Sevilla		las mejores		todas

Jaime and Paloma The French	are	the	most	polite logical	of all
The Americans			richest		
Seville oranges			best		

3

Aquél	es	mejor		que	el mío
Aquélla Éste		más	cara barato		la mía el tuyo
Ésta Ése Ésa		menos	buena raro grande		la tuya el suyo la suya
		un poco	más menos	pequeño	el nuestro la nuestra los míos las nuestras

That one (m) That one (f) This one (m)	is	better dearer cheaper		than	mine mine yours
This one (f)		less	good rare big		yours his* his
		a little	smaller less small		ours mine (pl) ours (pl)

* hers/yours/its. This will be the last reminder on this point.

4

Acabo	de	llegar	I	have	just	arrived
acabas		salir	You			gone out
acaba		entrar	He	has		come in
acabamos		ver a Juan	We	have		seen Juan
acaban		hablarle	They			spoken to him
		comprar vino				bought wine
		convidarle a casa				invited him home
		decirlo				said it

5

Dígame	qué hora es		Tell me	what time it is
dígale	cuántos discos tiene		him	how many records he has
díganos	por qué no quiere acompañarnos		us	why you don't want to come with us
dígales	cuándo llega el tren		them	when the train arrives

	que	soy guapo (-a)		that I	am handsome/pretty
		no soy rico (a)			am not rich
		no sé hablar español			don't know how to speak Spanish

EXPLANATIONS

1 Comparison of adjectives. The comparative of most adjectives is formed by placing *más* in front of them. Some have an irregular form:

bueno	good	*mejor*	better
malo	bad	*peor*	worse

2 Superlative forms are obtained by placing the definite article in front of the comparative:

El más alto	the tallest
La más delicada	the most delicate
El mejor pianista	the best pianist.

3 Demonstrative pronouns. We have met the demonstrative adjectives (*este libro*, 'this book') in Chapter 7. The pronouns, used of course without the noun, usually bear a written accent to distinguish them from the adjectives:

éste this one

4 Possessive pronouns. These correspond to the possessive adjectives in Chapter 7 and are preceded by the definite article:

El mío mine, my one

5 *Acabar de* literally means 'to finish doing something', but we normally say 'to have just done something'. *Acabamos de comer*—'we have just eaten'. Notice that it is followed by the infinitive.

6 *Poner* (to put) is an irregular verb.

Present tense:	*pongo*	*ponemos*	Gerund:	*poniendo*
	pones	*ponen*	Imperative:	*pon* (fam. s.)
	pone			*ponga* (polite s.)
				pongan (polite pl.)

7 *Salir* (to go out). A similar irregular verb.

Present tense:	*salgo*	*salimos*	Gerund:	*saliendo*
	sales	*salen*	Imperative:	*sal*
	sale			*salga*
				salgan

EXERCISES

Roberto y Federico están en el bar 'El Cordobés'. El coche de Roberto está enfrente del bar. Roberto es alto y delgado: Federico es pequeño y gordo. Paco está con ellos: es alto, pero menos alto que Roberto, y es gordo: más gordo que Federico.

Con ellos hay dos chicas, Teresa y Dolores, que acaban de llegar. Teresa es alta, pero no tan alta como Roberto: es guapísima y delgada. Dolores es un poquito menos alta, pero es gorda. Están esperando a Carmen.

Federico. —¿Cómo es tu amiga Carmen?

Teresa. —Es pequeña y muy delgada. Llega pronto.

1. ¿Quiénes están en el bar?
2. ¿Quién no está en el bar?
3. ¿Quiénes acaban de llegar?
4. ¿Quiénes son altos?
5. ¿Quién es el más alto de todos?
6. ¿Quién es el hombre más pequeño?
7. ¿Quién tiene coche?
8. ¿Quién es la chica más delgada?

Lección Diez

A El tren no está aquí   B pero llegará   C Saldrá a las
                           a las diez.   diez y cuarto.

LA EXCURSIÓN

Roberto: Mañana, como hay una excursión, ¿quieren acompañarnos?
Elena: Sí, con mucho gusto. ¿Adónde vamos?
Jaime: Primero, iremos al monasterio de San Pedro, que es una joya.
             Lo visitaremos, y veremos la capilla, que es preciosísima.
             También visitaremos la aldea, y verán Vds. los trajes típicos,
             porque es día de fiesta.
Roberto: Tocará las banda, y bailarán los aldeanos. No habrá lluvia,
             hará calor, y después de la comida echaremos una siesta.
Jaime: No, hombre, daremos un paseo.
Roberto: Bueno, tu darás un paseo y yo dormiré. Luego bajaremos a la
             aldea, bailaremos, cenaremos en la taberna, y volveremos muy
             tarde.
Ian: ¿A qué hora iremos?
Roberto: Tendrán que levantarse a las siete.
Elena: ¿Dónde está el monasterio?
Jaime: Está al norte, a dos horas de aquí.
Elena: Será una excursión muy larga.
Ian: Sí, y muy divertida.

acompañar – *to accompany*
iremos – *we shall go*
(*see E1.2*)
un monasterio – *monastery*
una joya – *jewel*
(*here 'a delight'*)
una capilla – *chapel*
una aldea – *village*
un aldeano – *villager*
el traje – *suit, costume*
típico – *typical*

el día de fiesta – *feast-day, holiday*
la banda – *band*
la lluvia – *rain*
la comida – *lunch*
echar la siesta – *to have an after-noon nap*
dar un paseo – *to go for a walk*
cenar – *to have dinner*
largo – *long*
divertido – *amusing, enjoyable*

FLUENCY PRACTICE

1a

visitaré	a Jaime		mañana
visitarás	al Sr Pérez		pasado mañana
visitará			
visitaremos	a	la madre de Juana	la semana que viene
visitarán		su hermana	el mes que viene
		España	el año que viene
veré		Madrid	dentro de dos días
verás		Londres	el tres
verá	el palacio		después de Navidad
veremos	el parque		en dos años
verán	las montañas		si no llueve demasiado

I	shall	visit	Jaime		tomorrow
you	will		Mr Pérez		the day after tomorrow
he			Juana's mother	next	week
we	shall		his sister		month
they	will		Spain		year
I	shall	see	Madrid		inside two days
you	will		London		on the third
he			the palace		after Christmas
we	shall		park		in two years
they	will		mountains		if it doesn't rain too much

1b

recibiré	una carta de mi madre
recibirás	flores de la parte del Sr Pérez
recibirá	una postal desde Alicante
recibiremos	mensajes del patrón
recibirán	un telegrama desde Nueva York

I	shall	receive	a letter from my mother
you	will		flowers from Mr Pérez
he			a postcard from Alicante
we	shall		messages from the boss
they	will		a telegram from New York

2

tendrán	alpargatas rojas	*They will*	*have*	*red rope-soled sandals*
harán	unos sombreros de paja		*make*	*some straw hats*
pondrán	camisas de seda		*put on*	*silk shirts*
	blusas de algodón			*cotton blouses*

3

me levantaré	temprano	*I shall get up*	*early*
te desayunarás	muy temprano	*you will breakfast*	*very early*
se marchará	por la tarde	*he will go away*	*in the evening*
nos afeitaremos	a las seis	*we shall shave*	*at six*
se lavarán	antes que tú	*they will get washed*	*before you*

4a

¿ Dónde está	Jaime?	Está	en	Sevilla
	el banco?			el pueblo
	la oficina?			un poquito más allá
	la aduana?			a dos kilómetros de aquí

Where is	*Jaime?*	*He's*	*in*	*Seville*
	the bank?	*It's*		*the town*
	the office?			*a little further along*
	the Customs?			*two kilometres away from here*

4b

¿ Adónde va Vd.?		*Where are you going?*	
Voy	a León	*I'm going*	*to León*
	a la ciudad		*to the town*
	más allá del río		*beyond the river*
	muy lejos de aquí		*very far from here*
	a buscar a mi mujer		*to look for my wife*

5

el	primer	día	saldremos de Londres
	segundo		llegaremos a Sevilla
	tercer		visitaremos la ciudad
	cuarto		iremos a Alicante
	quinto		llegaremos a Barcelona
	sexto		subiremos hasta Jaca
	séptimo		bajaremos hasta Zaragoza
	octavo		tomaremos el avión para Roma

On the	*first*	*day*	*we shall*	*leave London*
	second			*arrive in Seville*
	third			*visit the city*
	fourth			*go to Alicante*
	fifth			*arrive in Barcelona*
	sixth			*go up to Jaca*
	seventh			*go down to Zaragoza*
	eighth			*take the plane for Rome*

EXPLANATIONS

1 The future tense of regular verbs is formed by adding the endings *-é*, *-ás*, *-á*, *-emos*, *-án* to the infinitive. It is used to state what one intends to do or what will happen in the future when this is not so immediate as to need the form we have already met, the immediate future: *voy a salir* (I'm going to go out).

2 Irregular verbs tend to have irregular future tenses; but the endings are always regular: only the future stem sometimes differs from the infinitive; the first persons are listed here:

saber:	*sabré*	*querer:*	*querré*
tener:	*tendré*	*salir:*	*saldré*
hacer:	*haré*	*decir* (to say)*:*	*diré*
poder:	*podré*	*poner:*	*pondré*

The following act quite normally in this tense:

ser:	*seré*	*ir:*	*iré*
estar:	*estaré*	*dar:*	*daré*

Habrá (there will be) is the future of *hay* (there is, there are).

3 Named towns need the personal *a* when they are the object of a verb: *visitaré a París* 'I shall visit Paris'.

4 Some nouns ending in *-a* are masculine: *un problema* 'a problem', *un telegrama* 'a telegram'.

5 Some verbs change their meaning when made reflexive: *marchar* 'to walk', *marcharse* 'to go away'.

6 *¿ Dónde?* means 'where?', referring to a static object; when movement towards a place is meant, *¿ adónde . . . ?* must be used. *¿ Adónde va Pedro?* 'Where is Pedro going?'

7 *Primero* (abbreviated to *primer* in the example), *segundo*, etc. are ordinal numbers. As these are not needed for dates, they are rarely needed in everyday situations. Feminines: *primera, segunda, tercera, cuarta*, etc. (Guitar strings are *la prima, la segunda, la tercera, la cuarta, la quinta, el bordón*). *La primera clase*, 'first class', and *la segunda vez*, 'the second time' are common examples.

EXERCISES

1 Mañana Vd. tendrá que levantarse muy temprano para tomar el tren hasta Sevilla. El tren llega a las diez y media. En el tren Vd. quiere leer una novela española. El señor Covarrubias le espera a Vd. a las once en su casa. Él tiene que salir a las doce y media. Vd. comerá antes de volver.

 1. ¿A qué hora se levantará Vd. mañana?

 2. ¿Quedará Vd. aquí?

 3. ¿Irá Vd. a Sevilla en su coche?

 4. ¿Qué hará durante el viaje?

 5. ¿A qué hora llegará?

 6. ¿A qué hora verá al señor Covarrubias?

 7. ¿Cuánto tiempo tendrán para hablar?

 8. ¿Volverá Vd. a las doce y media?

2 Write out an itinerary of a journey with details of places to be visited, for yourself or other people, in the future tense.

A Jaime y Paloma llegan al restaurante.

B Jaime ha reservado una mesa.

C Ha pedido champán.

D La orquesta ha tocado muy bien.

E Han visto el espectáculo.

F Han bailado.

Jaime:	Mira, Paloma, te he traído estas flores.
Paloma:	Son maravillosas, Jaime.
Jaime:	Las he escogido para ti, Paloma. Oye, he reservado una mesa en el restaurante, cerca de la orquesta.
Paloma:	Eres perfecto, Jaime. ¡Ay, qué calor hace!
Jaime:	Hará fresco en el restaurante, y he pedido champán.

Paloma:	¡Estupendo!
	(*Entran en el restaurante*)
Paloma:	Es muy bueno el champán, Jaime. ¿Qué vamos a comer?
Jaime:	He pedido sandía, huevos, pollo con arroz, y helado.
Paloma:	Has escogido muy bien. Me gusta también la música. Es muy buena la orquesta.
Jaime:	Sí, es la que te ha gustado en el baile de Navidad.
Paloma:	¡Qué noche más perfecta!
Jaime:	Para después, he sacado entradas en el Teatro Nuevo, y luego iremos a bailar en el club donde hemos encontrado a Roberto, ¿sabes?
Paloma:	¡Qué hombre más perfecto!
Jaime:	¿Quién, Roberto?
Paloma:	No, tú, idiota.

un espectáculo – *show*
traído – *brought*
escoger – *to choose*
para – *for*
oye – *listen* (fam. s.)
ha reservado – *he has reserved*
 (*see E*1)
una mesa – *table*
una orquesta – *orchestra, band*
fresco – *cool, cold*
estupendo – *stupendous*
 (appreciative)

la sandía – *watermelon*
el pollo – *chicken*
el arroz – *rice*
la que – *the one* (*f.*) *which*
un baile – *dance*
sacar entradas – *to book seats*
 (*at theatre etc.*)
encontrar – *to meet*

FLUENCY PRACTICE

1

he	buscado	un libro interesante
has	comprado	una antología de cuentos
ha	escogido	una autobiografía
hemos	perdido	una biografía de Cervantes
han	leído	el 'Quijote' de Cervantes
	recibido	muchas novelas modernas

I have	*looked for*	*an interesting book*
you have	*bought*	*a collection of short stories*
he has	*chosen*	*an autobiography*
we have	*lost*	*a biography of Cervantes*
they have	*read*	*Cervantes' 'Don Quixote'*
	received	*many modern novels*

2

Ha sido	un gran placer	It	has been	a great pleasure	
	muy interesante	He	was	very	interesting
	muy amable				kind
	una experiencia inolvidable			an unforgettable experience	

3

He estado	muy satisfecho de todo	I have been	very pleased with everything
	enfermo, pero ahora estoy mejor	(was)	ill, but I am better now
	en la playa		on the beach
	varias veces en España		in Spain several times

4

Hemos hecho	todo para ayudarle	We	have done	everything to help him
	un viaje estupendo		did	a marvellous journey
	café para todo el mundo		have made	coffee for everybody
	un gran esfuerzo para llegar		made	a great effort to arrive
	temprano			early

5

Jorge	ha	ido	al banco
María		vuelto	para ver a su madre
Sr Martínez			muy tarde
el italiano			con la Sra Rodríguez

George	has	gone	to the bank
Mary		gone back	to see her mother
Mr Martínez	went		very late
the Italian	went back		with Mrs Rodríguez

6

¿ Ha visto	a Luis ? No, pero le he escrito
	mi novela ? Sí, Vd. la ha puesto debajo de su silla
	a mi madre ? No, no la he visto esta mañana
	a mi padre ? Sí, en el pueblo. No ha vuelto
	a su amigo ? No, no le he visto
	a los ingleses ? Sí, les he dicho que esperamos aquí

Have you seen	Luis ? No, but I've written to him
	my novel ? Yes, you put it under your chair
	mother ? No, I haven't seen her this morning
	father ? Yes, in town. He hasn't come back
	your friend ? No, I haven't seen him
	the Englishmen ? Yes, I told them we are waiting here

7

¿ Ha probado este plato?	No, me ha faltado apetito	
	Sí,	me ha gustado mucho
		pero no me ha gustado

Have you tried this dish?	No, I wasn't hungry	
	Yes,	I liked it a lot
		but I didn't like it

8

Ya	han	llegado	los amigos de Paco
		salido	los coches de los alemanes
		vuelto	sus padres
		desparecido	los limpiabotas
	se han ido		todos los pájaros

	have now	arrived
Paco's friends		left
The Germans' cars		returned
Your parents		disappeared
The bootblacks		gone away
All the birds		

9

¡Qué	hombre	más	fuerte!
	chica	tan	elegante!
	sitio		hermoso!
	flores		bonitas!

What	a	strong	man!
		smart	girl!
		beautiful	place!
		pretty flowers!	

10

Han	venido	caramelos	para	mí
	llegado	cartas		ti
		chocolates		él
		trajes		ella
		telegramas		Vd.
		uvas		nosotros
		periódicos		ellos
		noticias		ellos
		frutas		Vds.

Some	sweets	have	come	for	me
	letters		arrived		you (fam)
	chocolates				him
	dresses				her
	telegrams				you (pol)
	grapes				us
	papers				them (m)
	news	has			them (f)
	fruit				you (pl)

EXPLANATIONS

1 The perfect tense. This corresponds fairly closely to the English recent past tense (e.g. I have done) in formation and use. Occasions will be found on which it corresponds to other tenses, especially the simple past (e.g. I did).

The verb *Haber* ('to have'—but not denoting possession, for which *tener* is used) serves as an auxiliary: *he, has, ha, hemos, han* (I have, you have, etc.) This is placed before the past participle of the action verb.

The past participle ('done' etc.) of regular verbs is formed by removing the infinitive ending and replacing it by *-ado* for *-ar* verbs, and by *-ido* for *-er* and *-ir* verbs. *Fumar: fumado; comer: comido; recibir: recibido.*

2 Irregular forms. Many verbs which are regular in their other parts have irregular past participles: *escribir: escrito* and *abrir: abierto.*

Many irregular verbs have normal past participles: e.g. *saber: sabido; conocer: conocido; tener: tenido; poder: podido; querer: querido; dar: dado; ser: sido; estar: estado; salir: salido; traer: traído; leer: leído.* The stress mark on the last two is merely to show that it is the ending, not the stem, which is stressed.

Amongst irregular verbs with irregularly formed past participles are *hacer: hecho; ir: ido; ver: visto; volver: vuelto; decir: dicho; poner: puesto.*

3 The past participle is invariable: i.e. there is only one form, which does not show number or gender in any way.

4 In this tense, object pronouns and reflexive pronouns are placed before the auxiliary verb. *Lo he hecho* 'I have done it'; *las he visto* 'I have seen them'; *no le he encontrado* 'I haven't met him'. (Where one of these pronouns is the object of a verb in the infinitive, it follows it as usual: *no he podido hallarlo* 'I haven't been able to find it'.)

5 *Limpiabotas* (FP 8): this noun is invariable. It is made up from *limpiar* 'to clean' and *botas* 'boots'. As it refers to a man or boy, it is masculine. *Un limpiabotas* 'a bootblack'. A similar word is *un paraguas* 'an umbrella'.

6 The English 'What a . . . !' is expressed differently: the article is omitted, and *más* or *tan* used before the adjective: *¡Qué ciudad más hermosa!* 'What a beautiful town!'

EXERCISES

1 The person who made the journey detailed in Exercise 2 of the last chapter now writes an account of it in the perfect tense.

2 Answer the following using an object pronoun to refer to the thing or person mentioned, and the past tense.
Example: ¿No está aquí Paco? —Sí, le he visto.
1. ¿Dónde están mis amigos? No . . .
2. ¿Han llegado cartas para mí?
3. ¿Nos acompaña su madre?
4. ¿Quiere Vd. leer esta novela?

5. ¿Vd. no ha visto a las francesas?
6. ¿Ha probado este vino?
7. ¿Sus amigos han probado esto?
8. ¿Quiere Vd. venir a ver la película?

Lección Doce

Carmen: Son muy hermosas estas flores.

Paloma: Sí, me las dio Jaime anoche.

Carmen: Es hermosa. ¿ Has estado en Francia?

Paloma: Sí, la compré en París.

Carmen: ¿ Está aquí tu madre? Quiero hablar con ella.

Paloma: No está en casa; salió a las diez.

Carmen: Hola, Paloma, ¿qué tal?

Paloma: Muy bien, gracias, ¿y tú?

Carmen: Regular. No te veo mucho ahora.

Paloma: No, es que salgo mucho con Jaime. Anoche, por ejemplo, fuimos al restaurante, luego al teatro, y después bailamos casi toda la noche. Volví a casa a las cuatro de la madrugada—fue estupendo. Y tú, ¿qué haces?

Carmen: Yo nada, anoche me quedé en casa. Pero hace un mes fui a Francia con Mamá. Vimos la torre Eiffel, y las tiendas, y todo. Tenemos unos amigos franceses en el sur y fuimos a visitarles. Una vez nos llevaron en su coche hasta la playa.

Paloma: ¿Y qué tal te pareció Francia?

Carmen: Muy bien, pero todo es más caro que en España, ¿verdad?

Paloma: Sí, la primera vez que fui, me chocó. Pero me gustó el país, e hice muchas amistades. Sabes que conocí a Jaime en Francia?

Carmen: No, ¡qué raro!

Paloma: Sí, hija, le encontré en los Pirineos. No me gustó del todo, pero ahora me parece muy bien.

Carmen: Se ve, chica, se ve.

hermoso – *beautiful*	hace un mes – *a month ago*
anoche – *last night*	(*see E4*)
¡hola! – *hi!*	una torre – *tower*
¿Qué tal? – *how are you?*	en el sur – *in the south*
what's it like?	llevar – *to take, carry*
regular – *not bad*	la primera vez – *the first time*
por ejemplo – *for example*	chocar – *to shock*
fuimos – *we went*	hacer amistades – *to make friends*
(*see E1/2*)	hija, chica – *forms of address*
casi – *almost*	*between close*
la madrugada – *dawn* (here 'early	*girl friends*
morning')	¡qué raro! – *how strange!*
nada – *nothing*	los Pirineos – *the Pyrenees*
una casa – *house*	se ve – *that's obvious*
quedar – *to remain*	(*see E7*)
en casa – *at home*	

FLUENCY PRACTICE

1

hace	una semana dos meses tres siglos	viajé viajaste viajó	por	el norte toda España América
	mucho tiempo dos mil años	viajamos viajaron	hasta	Moscú Norteamérica

	A year *two months* *three centuries* *a long time* *two thousand years*	*ago*	*I* *you* *he* *we* *they*	*travelled*	*through the North* *throughout Spain* *through South America* *to Moscow* *to America*

2

anoche ayer anteayer	comí comiste comió	pescado ternera sopa	*last night* *yesterday* *the day before yesterday*	*I* *you* *he*	*ate*	*fish* *veal* *soup*
la semana pasada la última vez	comimos comieron	carne ensalada	*last week* * time*	*we* *they*		*meat* *salad*

en	enero febrero marzo abril mayo junio julio agosto setiembre octubre noviembre diciembre		verduras frutas habas guisantes	*in*	*January* *February* *March* *April* *May* *June* *July* *August* *September* *October* *November* *December*		*greens* *fruit* *beans* *peas*

3

cuando	llegué, llegaste, llegó, llegamos, llegaron,	te vi me hablaste le di noticias tuyas nos acostamos en seguida nos dijeron sus nombres y apellidos

	When	*I* *you* *he* *we* *they*	*arrived,*	*I saw you* *you spoke to me* *I gave him news of you* *we went straight to bed* *they told us their names*

76

4

Al	volar a España, comí churros y bebí vino tinto
	llegar al aeropuerto, escogiste una revista y la leíste
	salir del hotel, se despidió y subió en un tranviá
	tocar las nueve, subimos a la terraza para tomar refrescos

On	*returning to Spain, I ate 'churros'* and drank red wine*
	arriving at the airport, you chose a magazine and read it
	leaving the hotel, he said goodbye and got on a train
	the stroke of nine, we went up to the terrace to have refreshments

* A sort of long, thin doughnut

5

quise	subir a la cima	pero no	pude
quisiste	llegar a la playa		pudiste
quiso	ver al Sr Martínez		pudo
quisimos	hallar un río		pudimos
quisieron	acabar el libro		pudieron

I	*wanted to*	*go up to the top*	*but*	*I*	*couldn't*
you		*reach the beach*		*you*	
he		*see Mr Martínez*		*he*	
we		*find a river*		*we*	
they		*finish the book*		*they*	

6

tuve	suerte	*I*	*had*	*good luck*
tuviste	mucha suerte	*you*		*a lot of luck*
tuvo	poca suerte	*he*		*very little luck*
tuvimos	mala suerte	*we*		*bad luck*
tuvieron	tres horas para hacerlo	*they*		*three hours to do it*

7

vi	una película americana	pero no	me	gustó
viste	un espectáculo muy largo		te	
vio	una ópera italiana		le	
vimos	un baile clásico		nos	
vieron	todo el país		les	

I	*saw*	*a South American film*	*but*	*I*	*didn't like it*
you		*a very long show*		*you*	
he		*an Italian opera*		*he*	
we		*a classical ballet*		*we*	
they		*the whole country*		*they*	

77

EXPLANATIONS

1 The past definite tense (also called the preterite) corresponds roughly in use to the English tense known by the same names (also the simple past) e.g. I did, I went.

For regular verbs the following endings are added to the stem:

-ar: -é; -aste; -ó; -amos; -aron; e.g. *compré, compraste, compró, compraron:* (I bought etc.)

-er, -ir: -í, -iste, -ió, -imos, -ieron: e.g. *comí* (I ate), *comiste, comió, comimos, comieron* and *recibí,* (I received) etc.

2 In this tense, irregular verbs need careful attention as stems and stressing vary considerably from the regular pattern:

saber:	*supe, supiste, supo, supimos, supieron*
tener:	*tuve, tuviste, tuvo, tuvimos, tuvieron*
hacer:	*hice, hiciste, hizo* (*-z* because *-c-* not the right sound before *-o*) *hicimos, hicieron*
poder:	*pude, pudiste, pudo, pudimos, pudieron*
poner:	*puse, pusiste, puso, pusimos, pusieron*
querer:	*quise, quisiste, quiso, quisimos, quisieron*
estar:	*estuve, estuviste, estuvo, estuvimos, estuvieron*

(there is a similar pattern of stressing and endings in the above)

ser:	*fui, fuiste, fue, fuimos, fueron*
ir:	exactly the same as *ser*
ver:	*vi, viste, vio, vimos, vieron*
dar:	*di, diste, dio, dimos, dieron*
decir:	*dije, dijiste, dijo, dijimos, dijeron*

salir and *volver* are regular in this tense: *salí, volví* etc.

nacer: 'to be born' (an active verb in Spanish in spite of the English passive): *nací* 'I was born', etc.

3 Some orthographical changes are needed in this, as in other tenses, to keep the correct sound before certain endings. *Llegar* normally has the stem *lleg-* but needs the insertion of a *-u* before *-é* so as not to be pronounced *llej-*; *llegué*. Similarly *buscar* produces the first person *busqué*.

4 *Hace* and an expression of time means that much time ago.

5 *Nombres y apellidos* (FP 3). Spaniards commonly use the family names (*apellidos*) of the paternal and maternal lines, either placed together (*Pérez Galdós*) or joined by 'y' (*Martínez y Ruíz*). *Nombres* are first names.

6 *Al llegar* and similar expressions can be translated by 'on' and a noun

or present participle in English: on arrival, on arriving. If a subject is expressed, it follows: *al llegar el tren*, 'on the train's arrival'; *al llegar yo* 'when I arrived'.

7 *Se ve.* An example of the use of the reflexive as a sort of passive: 'that can be seen' (i.e. 'that's perfectly clear'). This is a widely used structure in Spanish. 'May I . . . ?' is often expressed by *¿ se puede . . . ?*

EXERCISES

1 1. ¿ En qué año nació Vd. ?
   2. ¿ Visitó Vd. España el año pasado ?
   3. ¿ Qué hizo Vd. ayer por la mañana ?
   4. Y el domingo pasado, ¿ qué hizo ?
   5. ¿ A qué hora llegó Vd. a casa anoche ?
   6. ¿ Dónde estuvo Vd. a las once ?
   7. ¿ Vd. vio una película esta tarde ?
   8. ¿ A qué hora salió Vd. de casa esta mañana ?

2 *Example:* Al llegar al río, paró su coche.
   1. Al llegar al café,   . . .
   2. Al acabar,   . . .
   3. Al salir del café,   . . .
   4. Al acostarme,   . . .
   5. Al levantarse,   . . .
   6. Al ver a la chica,   . . .

A Es ridículo el hombre que lleva dos sombreros.

B El chico que baila con Maite es muy guapo.

C El libro que lee Juan es muy interesante.

D El libro que está en la mesa está abierto.

E Paloma es la chica que más le gusta a Jaime.

F ¿Es el reloj que ha perdido Vd.?

Roberto: ¿Conoce Vd. a don Raimundo?

Ian: No he tenido este placer.

Roberto: Don Raimundo Pérez Torres, Ian Brown, un amigo nuestro. Don Raimundo es el señor que ha escrito el libro que te mostré ayer.

Ian: Me pareció muy interesante, y es un libro que quiero leer. ¿Ha escrito Vd. otros libros, Señor Pérez?

Sr Perez:	Sí, he escrito varios libros sobre problemas de nuestro tiempo, que le mandaré si le interesan.
Ian:	Vd. es muy amable. Será un gran placer para mí.
Roberto:	Don Raimundo tiene una finca cerca de San Pedro.
Ian:	¿Es el lugar que hemos visitado donde está el monasterio?
Roberto:	Eso es. Muchas de las tierras que hemos visto son de don Raimundo.
Ian:	Son muy hermosas.
Sr Perez:	(presenting his sister) ¿Conoce Vd. a mi hermana?
Ian:	Ah sí, es la señora con quien hablé en la aldea cuando me perdí.

llevar – *to carry, wear*
un chico – *boy*
abierto – *open*
perder – *to lose*
perderse – *to lose oneself*
un placer – *a pleasure*
mostrar – *to show* (radical changing verb *muestro* etc.)
escrito – *written* (irregular past participle)

varios – *various*
sobre – *about, on*
mandar – *to send*
interesar – *to interest*
una finca – *estate*
el lugar – *place, village*
eso es – *that's right*
la tierra – *land*
una aldea – *village*

FLUENCY PRACTICE

1

el coche	que	llegó anoche	es	inglés (inglesa)
la caravana		acaba de llegar	ha	venido desde París
el señor		hemos visto ayer	es	actor (actriz)
la señora		está delante del hotel		médico
		vieron miércoles		abogado
		vieron Jaime y Pedro		

	the	*car*	*which*	*arrived last night*	*is English*
		caravan		*has just arrived*	*has come from Paris*
		gentleman	*who*	*we saw yesterday*	*is*	*an actor*
		lady		*is in front of the hotel*		*a doctor*
				they saw on Wednesday		*lawyer*
				James and Pedro saw		

2

He	hallado visto	el libro la revista las gafas unas monedas	que	perdió Vd. ayer compró Vd. anoche dejó en el comedor me dio mi abuela
	encontrado	a la señora al guitarrista	a quien	vimos en Jaca hemos escuchado anoche

I have	found seen	the some	book magazine glasses coins	(which)	you lost yesterday bought last night left in the dining-room my grandmother gave me
	met	the	lady guitarist	(whom)	we saw in Jaca we listened to last night

3

El señor	Prat Torres Martínez Arias	que quien	ha venido para hablarnos, llegó hace unos minutos va a hablarnos de su pueblo ha escrito este libro	es	catalán navarrés aragonés castellano murciano leonés extremeño vasco madrileño sevillano barcelonés toledano

Mr	Prat Torres Martínez Arias	who	has come to speak to us arrived a few minutes ago is going to speak to us about his town/country has written this book	is	a Catalan from Navarre Aragonese a Castilian

	from	Murcia León Extremadura
	Basque	
	from	Madrid Seville Barcelona Toledo

4

| Jaime, | que | conociste en Soria | viene mañana |
| Luis,
Salvador,
Miguel, | a quien | ya has visto varias veces
encontró Paloma ayer
he convidado | vuelve esta tarde
no ha llegado
tiene seis hijas
es muy amable |

| | Jaime | whom | you knew in Soria | is coming tomorrow |
| | Luis
Salvador
Miguel | whom | you have now seen several times
Paloma met yesterday
I have invited to come | is coming back tonight
hasn't arrived
has six daughters
is very nice |

5

| María
Paloma
Dolores
Isabel | a quien | diste una rosa
mandé un telegrama
no has devuelto sus guantes
hemos ofrecido flores | te quiere mucho
no puede venir
no tardará en llegar
dice que está demasiado cansada para
bailar |

| | Maria
Paloma
Dolores | to whom | you | gave a rose
sent a telegram
haven't given back her gloves | loves you very much
can't come
won't be long arriving |
| | Isabel | | | we gave some flowers | says she is too tired
to dance |

6

| La | chica
mujer
francesa | con | quien | hablas todos los días
has bailado hace dos minutos
sale Juan
han llegado Vds. | es rica
ha desaparecido
no tiene padres
se ha ido | |
| | | para | | ha venido el coche
ha llegado un telegrama
he escogido este libro | es una amiga | nuestra
mía
suya |

| The | girl
woman
French girl | with | whom | you talk every day
you were dancing two minutes ago
Juan is going out
you arrived | is rich
has disappeared
has no parents
has gone | |
| | | for | | the car came
a telegram arrived
I chose this book | is a friend of | ours
mine
his |

EXPLANATIONS

1 Relative pronouns. *Que* refers to things or people, and can be subject or direct object; *quien* refers only to people and is a subject pronoun: to

use it as direct or indirect object it needs '*a*'; it can also be combined with *con* or *para*. The plural of *quien* is *quienes*; *que* is invariable.

2 The relative pronoun cannot be omitted, as it so often is in English. So: 'the man you saw': *el hombre que vio*; 'the girls you arrived with': *las chicas con quienes llegó*. The stilted English in the Fluency Practice results from a wish to conform to the Spanish pattern.

3 There is a nuance between *un amigo nuestro* and *nuestro amigo* corresponding to that between 'a friend of ours' and 'our friend'. The strong form of the possessive adjective (*mío, tuyo* etc.) is used after the noun.

4 Feminine of adjectives denoting locality or town: *catalán; catalana, aragonés; aragonesa*, etc.

EXERCISES

1 Translate:
    1. She is the girl who arrived last night.
    2. The man who was singing all night is leaving today.
    3. They arrived in the car which is in front of ours.
    4. The lady you saw this morning hasn't many friends.
    5. That's the girl Carlos sent some flowers to.
    6. The Swedish girls (las suecas) we were talking to last night are going to Pamplona.
    7. The seats we like are reserved.
    8. That's the man the telegram came for yesterday.

2 Read Chapter 7 over again, and answer these questions:
    1. ¿De quién habla Jaime?
    2. ¿Con quiénes habla?
    3. ¿A quién ha dado una corbata Roberto?
    4. ¿A quiénes escribirá Jaime?
    5. ¿A quién va a mandar flores?

3 Make up similar questions and answers, using the different tenses studied, for other past lessons.

A Cuando yo era joven,   B bailaba mucho.

C Cuando yo era joven,   D jugaba mucho al fútbol.

Luis:	¿Te acuerdas del día que pasamos a Blanes?
Maite:	Sí, claro, ¡qué día más espléndido! Brillaba el sol, había pocas nubes en el cielo, hacía calor pero no demasiado, el mar estaba caliente: todo era perfecto.
Luis:	Y tú llevabas ese traje que me gusta mucho, ¿sabes? con flores rojas sobre fondo blanco.
Maite:	Sí, me gustaba mucho.
Luis:	¿Así que no lo tienes todavía?
Maite:	Está manchado. Lo llevaba el otro día, estaba escribendo una carta a mi hermano, y dejé caer la tinta. No faltaba más.
Luis:	Por lo menos tengo una foto en que se ve.
Maite:	¿Ah? ¿Cuándo la sacaste?

Luis: Cuando yo iba con Jaime para comprar cigarrillos, y tú andabas en la playa con Paloma.

Maite: Nunca he visto las fotos que hiciste aquel día.

Luis: Son muy buenas. Saqué una cuando dormías, y otras cuando te bañabas en el mar. Podrás verlas esta tarde.

joven – *young*
¿ te acuerdas ? – *do you remember ?*
brillaba – *was shining*
la nube – *cloud (see E1)*
el cielo – *sky*
caliente – *hot*
llevabas – *you were wearing*
el fondo – *background*

blanco – *white*
roja – *red*
manchado – *stained*
la tinta – *ink*
no faltaba más – *that's all I needed*
(lit. no more was needed)
por lo menos – *at least*
bañarse – *to bathe*

FLUENCY PRACTICE

1

andaba	(muy)	despacio	porque	estaba cansado (-a)
nadaba		de prisa		tenía que ir lejos
bailaba		energicamente		quería impresionar a todo el mundo
saltaba				hacía frío
				calor

I was	*walking*	*(very)*	*slowly*	*because*	*I was tired*
he	*swimming*		*quickly*		*he had a long way to go*
she	*dancing*		*energetically*		*she wanted to impress everybody*
	jumping				*it was* *cold*
					hot

2a

¿ cantabas	mucho			cuando	eras	niño ?
¿ tocabas		el piano				niña ?
		la guitarra				joven ?
¿ jugabas		al	tenis		tenías	ocho años ?
			fútbol			diez
		a la pelota				once
¿ viajabas						

Did you	*sing*			*very much*	*when*	*you were*	*a child ?*
	play	*the*	*piano*				*young ?*
			guitar				
		tennis					*eight ?*
		football					*ten ?*
		pelota					*eleven ?*
	travel						

2b

¿ estabas	en casa		cuando	llegué?
	en el	jardín		llamé por teléfono?
		cuarto de baño		vine?

	Were you	in the	house garden bathroom	when	I	arrived? telephoned? came?

3

iba ibas íbamos iban	al	club teatro	en aquel momento antes de conocer a María		
		cine	cuando	tenía tenías teníamos tenían	tiempo para ello que hacerlo ganas de hacerlo que ir
	a la	escuela biblioteca iglesia universidad			

I used to go he was going	to the	club theatre	at that time before getting to know María			
she you were going		cinema school	when	I he	had	time for it to do it
we they		library church		she you we	felt like it had to go	
		university		they		

4

estaba andaba iba	bailando cantando riéndose de nosotros llorando gritando arrojando piedras comiendo uvas bebiendo botella tras botella de vino	He was he was going along he was going along	dancing singing laughing at us crying shouting throwing stones eating grapes drinking bottle after bottle of wine

87

5

al llegar	(yo), (tú), (la policía), (nosotros), (los guardias),	vi dijiste notaron nos apercibimos pudieron ver	que	no estaba ya comían estaba borracho arrojaba vasos no se pasaba nada bailaban en la calle les amenazaba un perro enorme
When	I you the police we the Civil Guard	arrived,	I saw you said they noticed we noticed they could see	that	he wasn't there they were already eating he was drunk he was throwing glasses nothing was happening they were dancing in the street a huge dog was threatening them

EXPLANATIONS

1 The imperfect tense expresses past actions which were unfinished at the time, repeated, or habitual. English translations vary: did (often, repeatedly,) was doing, used to do . . . It also describes past states, and contrasts with the past definite: *llovía cuando llegué* 'it was raining when I arrived'.

2 It is formed for regular verbs by adding the following endings to the stem:

-ar: -aba, -abas, -aba, -ábamos, aban;
-er, -ir: -ía, -ías, -ía, -íamos, -ían.

3 Most irregular verbs form the imperfect as if they were regular verbs. The only exceptions from the selection of irregular verbs used so far in this book are:

ser: *era, eras, era, éramos, eran*
ir: *iba, ibas, iba, íbamos, iban*
ver: *veía, veías, veía, veíamos, veían*

dar works regularly, the stem being *d-: daba*, etc.

4 To add extra weight to the fact that the action of a verb was continuing at a certain time, the imperfect of *estar* and the gerund of the action verb ('doing') are often used. *Estaba quemando* 'it was burning'. (This is equivalent to turning the present continuous *está quemando* 'it is burning' into the imperfect). *Andar* or *ir* plus a gerund can be used (a) literally, to mean someone was going along doing something, and (b) figuratively, to show they went on doing it.

5 *Tener* (FP 2) is used idiomatically with a duration to give someone's age. *Tiene dos meses* 'he's two months old'.

6 'To be here' or 'to be there' (FP 5), in various tenses, can be rendered in Spanish without a word for 'here' or 'there' when the context makes the meaning clear. Thus, calling at a house *¿está el Señor Hernández?* 'is Señor H. in?' or 'I called but he wasn't there' *llamé pero no estaba*.

EXERCISES

1 Todos los días, el señor Martínez bajaba a las ocho; bebía chocolate y ... (this is the methodical man from Chapter 5: go on with his day in the imperfect tense.)

2 Cuando Vd. era niño/niña, ¿jugaba mucho?
¿tocaba el piano?
¿iba al cine?
¿tenía muchos amigos?
¿vivía en Leeds?
¿le gustaban los caramelos?
¿cantaba mucho?
¿sabía hablar español?

3 ¿Qué tiempo hacía a las ocho?
anoche a las nueve?
ayer a las once de la mañana?
cuando Vd. volvió de vacaciones?

4 *Example:* Estaba en la cantina cuando llegó el tren.
Complete the following, using the imperfect tense:
1. ... cuando llegaron sus amigos.
2. Cuando le hallaron, ...
3. Cuando llegó el avión, ...
4. Todas las noches ...
5. Cuando le vieron en la playa, ...
6. Por la mañana ...
7. Se bañaba en el mar ...
8. Antes de conocerle a Vd. ...

Lección Quince

A ¿Quiere Vd. bailar?

B Me gustaría pero no puedo.

C Me gustaría comprarlo,

D pero no me queda dinero.

Ian: ¿Vd. vendrá a Londres el año próximo?

Don Raimundo: No sé si podré, pero me gustaría.

Ian: Podríamos visitar juntos todos los sitios agradables, los parques, los museos, los almacenes, los teatros . . .

Don Raimundo: Esto me interesaría muchísimo. Tendré que ver: espero que podré pasar una semana o dos en Inglaterra. Había esperado volver a Londres el año pasado, pero resultó imposible. La última vez que estuve en Inglaterra fue en el sesenta y nueve.

Ian: ¿Ah? No sabía que Vd. había estado en Inglaterra.

Don Raimundo: Ah sí, me gusta mucho su país.

Ian: Pues ya habrá visto a Londres.

Don Raimundo: Claro, pero queda mucho que ver. Me habría gustado pasar días enteros en el British Museum, pero no pude.

Ian: ¡Qué bien le comprendo! A mí me pasa igual con el Prado.
Me habría quedado un mes entero.

quedar algo – *to have something remaining, left (see E5)*	un museo – *museum*
juntos – *together*	un almacén – *store*
agradable – *pleasant*	resultar – *to turn out to be*
un parque – *park*	último – *last*
	entero – *whole*
	igual – *the same*

FLUENCY PRACTICE

1

En este caso	tendría mucho que ver	*In that case*	*I'd have a lot to see*
	no llamaría		*I wouldn't call*
	iría al baile con Maite		*I'd go to the dance with Maite*
	no sabría hacerlo		*I wouldn't know how to do it*
	tendría ganas de hacerlo		*I'd want to do it*
	lo haría		*I'd do it*
	podría venir		*I'd be able to come*
	volvería al día siguiente		*I'd come back next day*
	vería Vd. al Sr Rojas		*you'd see Mr Rojas*
	estaría muy contento		*I'd be very happy*
	diríamos que estaba enfermo		*we'd say that he was ill*
	no bailaría más		*I wouldn't dance any more*

2

había	vuelto	cuando	llamaron a la puerta
habías	salido		llegó tu amigo
habíamos	dado una vuelta		nos vieron
habían	pagado al chófer		salió el tren
	visto a tu amigo	antes de	cenar
	ido al cine		encontrarse*
	estado en el agua		despedirse*
	querido verte		

* -me, -te, *etc.*

I, he, etc. had	*returned*	*when*	*they knocked at the door*
you	*gone out*		*your friend arrived*
we	*gone for a walk*		*they saw us*
they	*paid the driver*		*the train left*
	seen your friend	*before*	*having dinner*
	gone to the cinema		*meeting*
	been in the water		*saying goodbye*
	wanted to see you		

3

habré	comido	antes de	venir
habrás	cenado		llegar
habrá	visto al dueño		empezar
habremos	reparado el coche		salir para Granada
habrán	arreglado el tocadiscos		ir a casa de Carlos

I	shall	have	eaten, had lunch	before	coming
you	will		eaten, had dinner		arriving
he			seen the owner		starting
we			repaired the car		leaving for Granada
they			fixed the record player		going to Carlos'

4

De haber sabido que	no tenías discos	te habría traído unos
	estabas enfermo	no habría venido
De haberlo sabido		habríamos llamado antes
		habría convidado a Jaime
		habrían dejado algo
		habríamos podido llegar más temprano

If I had known	you	hadn't any records	I'd have brought some
		were ill	I wouldn't have come
If we had known (it)			we'd have called before
			I'd have invited Jaime
			they'd have left something
			we could have got here earlier

5

no	me	queda	tiempo	I	haven't	enough time left	
	te		dinero	you		any	money	left
	le		tinta	he	hasn't		ink	
	nos		gasolina	we	haven't		petrol	
	les	quedan	sobres	they			envelopes	
			sellos				stamps	
			patatas				potatoes	

6

no	he visto	nada	I haven't seen	anything
	tenía		He didn't have	
	verá		He won't see	
	habrá vendido		He won't have sold	

7

no	llegó	nadie	Nobody	arrived
	lo hizo			did it
	pudo hacerlo			could do it
	la conoce			knows her

8

no hemos	visto hallado invitado	a	nadie	We haven't	seen found invited	anybody
	hablado salido	con			spoken to gone out with	

9

no	vino llegó	nunca		he	never	came arrived
	llegará			he'll		arrive
	los come lo bebe			he		eats them drinks it

EXPLANATIONS

1 The conditional tense expresses what would happen under certain conditions, and is formed like the future but with the following set of endings: *-ía, -ías, -ía, -íamos, -ían. De tener bastante dinero, compraría aquel coche* 'If I had enough money, I'd buy that car.' (N.B. use the future stem for irregular verbs, *ser: sería* 'I would be', *querer: querría* 'I would want', etc.)

2 The pluperfect expresses what had already happened at a given moment, and is formed by using the imperfect tense of *haber* with the past participle of the action verb: *habían acabado cuando llegué* 'they had finished when I arrived'.

3 a) The future perfect (what will have happened) is formed by using the future of *haber* (*habré*, etc.) with the past participle of the verb: *habré acabado dentro de unos minutos* 'I shall have finished within a few minutes'.
b) The future perfect is also used to express probability where the English is 'probably' and perfect tense. *Vd. habrá visto este libro* 'you've probably seen this book'.

4 The conditional perfect (what would have happened) is formed by using the conditional of *haber* (*habría*, etc.) with the past participle: *habría acabado* 'I would have finished'.

5 *Quedar* 'to remain', can be used like *gustar* and *faltar* (i.e. impersonally): *no me queda tinta* 'I have no ink left'.

6 Negatives like *nada* 'nothing', *nunca* 'never', *nadie* 'nobody', can be placed before the verb (*nada ocurre* 'nothing is happening', *nunca viene* 'he never comes' *nadie lo sabe* 'nobody knows') or used after a normal

93

negative verb: *no ocurre nada, no viene nunca, no lo sabe nadie.* Differentiate between *no ha visto nadie* (nobody saw) and *no ha visto a nadie* (he didn't see anyone).

EXERCISES

1 Complete the following, using the conditional tense:
   Example: De estar aquí Luis, bailaría con Carmen.
   1. De estar aquí Carmen, . . .
   2. De no estar cansado, . . .
   3. De tener hambre, . . .
   4. De tener bastante dinero, . . .
   5. De estar aquí su amigo, . . .
   6. De no estar aquí su amigo, . . .

2 Complete the following using the future perfect tense:
   Example: Antes de llegar Jaime, habré acabado la carta.
   1. Antes de llegar a Córdoba, . . .
   2. Antes de bajar a la playa, . . .
   3. Antes de entrar en el cine, . . .
   4. Antes de dejar a Juan, . . .
   5. Antes de subir en el avión, . . .
   6. Antes de pagar al dueño, . . .

3 Translate into Spanish:
   1. He never had enough time left.
   2. She's always losing things but never finds anything.
   3. Nobody comes here on Tuesdays.
   4. I've never seen anyone here on Tuesday.
   5. He'll never come back.
   6. Nobody likes that.

Lección Dieciséis

A Quiero que me dé más dinero.

B No quiero que te vayas.

C Quiero que anden más despacio.

D No permito que Vd. entre.

María:	No quiero que te vayas, Henry.
Henry:	Yo tampoco quiero irme, María. Pero es preciso. ¿Tienes una foto tuya?
María:	Sí, tengo aquí una que he traído para ti. Y quiero que me des una foto tuya.
Henry:	Te la mandaré en una carta.
María:	Escribirás mucho, ¿verdad?
Henry:	Claro que sí, querida. Te escribiré todos los días. Quiero que siempre te acuerdes de mí.
María:	No me imagino cómo es tu vida.
Henry:	Cuando vengas a Inglaterra lo verás.
Luisa y Carmencita (las hermanitas de María):	¿Y nos escribirás también?

Henry: Sí, os escribiré y mandaré muñequitas. Y a Vd. también le escribiré, Señor Valdés. No quiero que se olviden Vds. de mí.

Sr Valdés: No queremos tampoco que se olvide de nosotros, ni de España. Buen viaje de regreso, y espero que volverá a España.

Henry: Vd. puede estar seguro de que no tardaré en volver. Vds. han sido magníficos. ¡Adiós! ¡Hasta la vista!

no quiero que te vayas – *I don't want you to go away* (*see E*1)

tampoco – *neither*

es preciso – *it is necessary* (*see E*1c)

la hermanita – *little sister*

os – *you* (*see E*3)

olvidar – *to forget*

una muñequita – *doll*

el regreso – *return*

¡Hasta la vista! – *Till we meet again!*

FLUENCY PRACTICE

1

(No) quiero que		*I (don't) want*		
	te vayas		you to	go away
	se vaya		him	
	se vayan		them	
	estés triste		you to	be sad
	me dejes			leave me
	me olvides			forget me
	bebas demasiado			drink too much
	bailes con Dolores			dance with Dolores
	creas esto			believe that
	vivas lejos de aquí			live a long way from here
	andes tan de prisa			walk so quickly
	lleves el coche			drive the car
	pagues			pay

2

Es preciso		*You must*	
	darte prisa (que te dés prisa)		hurry up
	irte (que te vayas)		go away
	andar de prisa (que andes de prisa)		walk quickly
	ver al dueño (que veas al dueño)		see the owner

3

| Dígale que
Pídale | (no) | se vaya
nos deje
me traiga más cerveza
lo escriba en este papel

nos llame por teléfono mañana
arregle el coche lo más pronto posible
espere
esté aquí antes de las nueve
vaya a buscar otro mejor
salga de aquí
vuelva mañana
me dé sus señas
ponga esto en mi cuenta | Tell him
Ask him | (not) | to | go away
leave us
bring me more beer
write it down on this paper
ring up tomorrow
fix the car as soon as possible
wait
be here before nine
go and find a better one
get out of here
come back tomorrow
give me his/her address
put this on my bill |

4

| No creo que
Quizás
Tal vez
Ojalá | sea él
llegue tan pronto
lo tengan aquí
venga Juan
esto se pueda hacer
lo haya hecho hoy | I don't believe
Perhaps
Perhaps
I do hope | it's him
he'll arrive so soon
they have it here
Juan is coming
this can be done
he's done it today |

5

¿ Quieres	este libro? esta corbata?	Do you Does he	want	this	book? tie?
	estos periódicos? estas uvas?	Do they Does Paco		these	newspapers? grapes?
¿ Quiere ¿ Quieren ¿ Quiere Paco					

| Pues | te
se | lo
la
los
las | doy | Then I'll give | it
them | to | you
him
her
you (pol.)
them |

97

Si se	lo la	pides, tendrá que	dártelo dártela
	los las		dártelos dártelas

	If you ask him for	*it,*	*he will have to give*	*it*	*to you*
		them		*them*	

EXPLANATIONS

1 The tenses so far studied have been in the indicative mood, with the exception of the commands which are in the imperative mood. The subjunctive mood, not very common in English, is an essential part of the Spanish language, and the present tense is needed for many common expressions.

Regular verbs form their present subjunctive by putting the *-er, -ir* endings of the present indicative on to the *-ar* stems and vice versa, thus:

hablar: hable, hables, hable, hablemos, hablen
comer: coma, comas, comas, comamos, coman
recibir: reciba, recibas, reciba, recibamos, reciban

Irregular verbs:

   estar stresses the ending in the present subjunctive as it does in the indicative: *esté, estés, esté, estemos, estén*

tener: tenga, tengas, tenga, tengamos, tengan
salir: salga, etc.
traer: traiga, etc.
decir: diga, etc.
poner: ponga, etc.
hacer: haga, etc.

Others from our list are as follows:

saber:	sepa	poder:	pueda	ir:	vaya
conocer:	conozca	querer:	quiera	ver:	vea
haber:	haya	ser:	sea	volver:	vuelva (*volvamos*)
dar:	dé, des, dé, demos, den				

Some of these forms have been met as the polite imperative of certain verbs.

Examples given here as an introduction to the use of the Spanish present subjunctive are as follows:

a) *No te vayas*   Don't go away (All negative
                                    commands are actually subjunctive)

b) *Quiero que te vayas*   I want you to go away
    No quiero que te vayas   I don't want you to go away

The construction *quiero irme* (I want to go away), *quieres irte* (You want to go away) can only be used when both verbs have the same subject.

Quiere que me vaya   he/she/it wants, you want me to go away

Quieres que se vaya   you want him/her/it to go away

c) 'To be necessary'. This can be expressed either as in the English, by the infinitive:

Es preciso darse prisa   It is necessary to hurry

or by the subjunctive:

Es preciso que te des prisa   You must hurry up (lit. 'it is necessary that you should hurry')

d) After a statement of disbelief, the verb is in the subjunctive mood.

    No creo que sea él   I don't think it is him

(not *es él*, because this is untrue or believed to be untrue).

e) *¡Ojalá!* (an expression equivalent to 'Pray God that . . . !'
    ¡Ojalá sea él!   I do hope it is him (lit. 'Pray God that it is him!)

f) *Quizás, tal vez* (perhaps). Followed by the indicative if you feel that it is very probable (*quizás es él*); but by the subjunctive if you are almost sure it is not (*quizás sea él*).

g) *Dígale que se vaya* (tell him to go away). When one person is to tell another to do something, the verb needs to be in the subjunctive.

h) *Cuando vengas* (when you come). The present subjunctive is used after *cuando* if the action is in the future.

2 Two object pronouns. *Me lo da* (he gives it to me).

The indirect object pronoun precedes the direct object pronoun.

Me, te, nos, os (see below) precede normally, but the expected combination with *le* does not occur; the third person indirect object pronoun followed by the direct object pronoun becomes *se: se lo, se la, se los, se las.*

When pairs of pronouns follow the infinitive, they are written as one word with it, and the stress is modified to keep it in the normal place.

    Quiero dar un libro a Juan   I want to give a book to Juan
    Quiero darle un libro   I want to give him a book
    Quiero dárselo   I want to give it to him.

3 *Os*. This is the object pronoun plural corresponding to *te* in the singular. It is familiar.

The corresponding subject pronoun is *vosotros, vosotras* (you, subject familiar plural). The condition for this form of address is that both or all of the people being addressed would be addressed by *tú* individually. (If one out of a pair or group is normally addressed as *Vd.*, then *Vds.* is to be used.)

The second person plural form of the verb in the indicative or subjunctive usually ends in *-áis* or *-éis*. The command form ends in *-ad*, *-ed*, *-id*.

	Pr. Indic.	Pret.	Imperf.	Future	Conditional
llamar:	llamáis	llamásteis	llamábais	llamaréis	llamaríais
comer:	coméis	comístais	comíais	comeréis	comeríais
recibir:	recibís	recibísteis	recibíais	recibiréis	recibiríais

	Imperative	Present subjunctive
	llamad	llaméis
	comed	comáis
	recibid	recibáis

For the irregular verbs encountered in this book, putting the regular ending on to the appropriate tense stem will normally give the correct form, except for *ser: sois* (pr. indic.); *sed* (imperative).

EXERCISES

1 Translate:
1. I don't want you to stay.
2. He wants her to stay.
3. They want him to come on Thursday.
4. She doesn't want him to dance with Isabel.
5. It's necessary for you to talk to him.
6. They don't believe that he has enough money.
7. Perhaps he will arrive before eleven o'clock—but it would be the first time.
8. I don't believe you want him to come.

2 Rewrite the wishes in the main dialogue of Chapter 16 in the third person (María no quiere . . . , etc.).

3 Complete the following using appropriate tenses and object pronouns
(e.g. María buscaba su revista cuando la vi hace dos horas. —La tenía
yo, pero ya se la he vuelto).

1. Tu hijo lloraba porque quería caramelos,   . . .
2. El señor Martínez ha perdido su reloj de oro.   . . .
3. A Dolores le gustarían muchísimo estas flores.   . . .
4. De haberme pedido el libro,   . . .
5. A mi madre le gusta recibir noticias mías, pues   . . .
6. Roberto mira siempre esta corbata pues   . . .

Index